A SUSSEX GUIDE

THE LONG MAN & FRIENDS
SACRED SUSSEX

PHILIP CARR-GOMM
&
DAVID BRAMWELL

Illustrated by
IVAN HISSEY

SNAKE RIVER PRESS

SNAKE RIVER PRESS

Book No 23
Books about Sussex for the enthusiast

Published in 2025 by
SNAKE RIVER PRESS
an imprint of Anness Publishing Ltd
snakeriverpress.co.uk; annesspublishing.com; info@anness.com

ISBN 978-1-906022-32-7

© Snake River Press Limited / Anness Publishing Ltd 2025
Text © Philip Carr-Gomm & David Bramwell

All rights reserved. No part of this publication may be reproduced, stored in a retrieval system, or transmitted in any way or by any means, electronic, mechanical, photocopying, recording or otherwise, without the prior written permission of the copyright holder.

A CIP catalogue record for this book is available from the British Library.

The publishers and authors have done their best to ensure the accuracy and currency of all information at the date of preparation. Readers who intend to rely on the information to undertake any activity should check the current accuracy. The publishers and authors accept no responsibility for any loss, injury or inconvenience sustained by the reader as a result of information or advice contained in this book.

ART DIRECTOR & PUBLISHER *Peter Bridgewater*
PAGE MAKEUP *Richard Constable*
ILLUSTRATOR *Ivan Hissey*
EDITOR *Caroline Earle*

This book is typeset in Perpetua & Gill Sans,
two fonts designed by Eric Gill

Printed in China

DEDICATION

For Stephanie & Anne

CONTENTS

INTRODUCTION 6

PART ONE
**A GAZETTEER OF
SACRED SITES IN SUSSEX** *13*

CHALK GODS *19*

SACRED STONES *19*

HOLY WATERS *22*

MAGICAL TREES *24*

PILGRIM PATHS *28*

ANCIENT SETTLEMENTS *31*

BARROWS, TUMULI & TUMPS *34*

SACRED BUILDINGS,
HOMES & COMMUNITIES *39*

SUSSEX VISIONARIES *50*

PART TWO
**NINE WALKS EXPLORING THE
MAGIC LANDSCAPE OF SUSSEX** . .*55*

WALK 1
HILLFORTS & HIDDEN GEMS
*Cissbury Ring &
Highdown Gardens* *56*

WALK 2
ANCIENT YEWS & HILLTOP BARROWS
*From Kingley Vale
to the Devil's Humps* *59*

WALK 3
A MEDITATION ON MORTALITY
AT THE MARGINS OF BRIGHTON
The Chattri & Clayton Tunnel *63*

WALK 4
A MEDITATIVE MEANDER
THROUGH MONASTIC WOODS
Chithurst Monastery & Lakeside *66*

WALK 5
FROM HIGH ROCKS
TO HEALING WATERS
High Weald & Tunbridge Wells *69*

WALK 6
WEAVING THE ANCESTORS' VOICES
*The Long Man of Wilmington
& Berwick Church* *73*

WALK 7
SACRED WATERS OF HASTINGS
Alexandra Park to St Helen's Woods . .*78*

WALK 8
THE OCCULT MYSTERIES OF SUSSEX
Steyning & Chanctonbury Ring *83*

WALK 9
A PLEIADES PILGRIMAGE
Up on the Lewes Downs *88*

TIPS FOR SAFE WALKING *92*

ACKNOWLEDGEMENTS
& RESOURCES *94*

INDEX *95*

INTRODUCTION

*'And, in her secret heart,
The heathen kingdom Wilfrid found
Dreams, as she dwells, apart'*
RUDYARD KIPLING

SUSSEX – less than an hour from London – but so wild! It's the most goblin-haunted part of Britain: thirteen names in the county derive from puca, which means goblin. It is where the Devil's wife is buried (at Devil's Dyke) and where the last of the fairies to survive in southern England live (at Harrow Hill near Burpham say some, at Burlow Castle in the Cuckmere Valley say others). It is also where the dragons of Knucker Hole or St Leonard's Forest might eat you up, and where the giants of Firle, Caburn or Windover might challenge you to a stone hurling contest. And it is where the ghostly sound of the Bronze Age trumpet, the dord, can be heard near Battle.

Come to Lewes on Bonfire Night, get lost in the yew forest of Kingley Vale as the sun goes down, trek along the coastal path or across Ashdown Forest, and you can still feel the pagan heart of Sussex beating. According to the Anglo-Saxon scholar the Venerable Bede, it was the last county in Britain to convert to Christianity.

Access from the north was hard. The great Waste of Ondred that stretched across Sussex in the flatlands between the North and South Downs was dangerous: wolves, bears and brigands roamed the forest. Malaria was rife in the swampy marshlands. And as for access from the south, when St Wilfrid and his missionaries arrived on the Sussex coast in the rather inauspicious year of 666, determined to convert the locals, they found themselves instead attacked by them. After losing five men, Wilfrid's mission managed to escape and sail on to Kent, receiving a more friendly reception in Sandwich. It took another fifteen years before Wilfrid could return to convert the area, with Sussex's first Christian ruler King Æðelwealh donating land to him at Selsey for the building of a church, which would become Selsey Abbey. Its location

INTRODUCTION

is no longer known. Some say it was on land now under the sea, and on rough nights you can hear its bell tolling beneath the waves.

Though Sussex had become nominally Christian by the end of the 7th century, not all the old ways were lost. Brian Bates, a psychology professor at Sussex University in the 1980s, became so intrigued by the way Christianity and earlier spiritual practices became woven together in this region, he used the spells and rituals for healing that he found in an Anglo-Saxon manuscript as the basis for his book *The Way of Wyrd* (1983) – a fictional account of the relationship between a Christian missionary newly arrived in Sussex and an Anglo-Saxon wizard.

Bates' story was no mere fantasy, the manuscript that inspired him combined Christian and pre-Christian influences in a way that is echoed in the landscape here. The early Christians built their churches in the places that were already hallowed as sacred before they arrived. In 601 Pope Gregory wrote in a letter: 'I have, upon mature deliberation of the affair of the English, determined ... that the temples of the idols in those nations ought not to be destroyed; but let the idols that are in them be destroyed; let holy water be made and sprinkled in the said temples, let altars be erected, and relics placed. For if those temples are well built, it is requisite that they be converted from the worship of devils to the service of the true God; that the nation, seeing that their temples are not destroyed ... may the more familiarly resort to the places to which they are accustomed.' And so we see places like Berwick in East Sussex where the church is tucked beside an ancient barrow, or in nearby Lullington where the tiniest church has been built within what was probably a sacred grove. Sitting in these old Sussex churches, you can feel the power of worship and tradition coming from way back – from before the time the stones were laid and the altars erected.

This fusing of old and newer influences continues. For a number of years, until the gatherings became so popular they proved unwieldy, members of the Anglican congregation of Firle would join with local druids, Wiccans, pagans and other folk to celebrate the solstices on

Firle Beacon — in the eye of the sun and under the watchful gaze of those ancestors whose remains were laid to rest in the barrows by the Beacon all those centuries ago.

And today the sacred landscape of Sussex is enriched not only by 1,400 years of Christian influence, with its churches and graveyards and stories of local saints and miracles keeping the flames of reverence and tradition alive in our materialistic society, but also by the presence of other religions and approaches to the sacred — reflecting the multicultural nature of Britain today.

———

Although the big solstice gatherings no longer occur on Firle Beacon, the full cycle of eight seasonal celebrations of the solstices and equinoxes and four Celtic fire festivals have been celebrated as events open to all beneath the Long Man of Wilmington for over twenty years by a local druid group — the Anderida Gorsedd. After each celebration, participants descend on the Long Man Inn for refreshments, which explains the certificate displayed on its wall, declaring it the most druid-friendly pub in Sussex.

Both of the authors of this book know the organisers of these rituals, and on a winter's evening, a few years back, one of us got involved in a rather more private rite they had planned. This illustrates the degree to which the land beneath our feet can become a source of spiritual inspiration:

I'm in a sitting room crammed full of people in Southwick, a small town just outside Brighton. It's 8 o'clock in the evening on the night of the winter solstice. There's a bustle and plenty of laughter, but there's serious work afoot. My partner Stephanie and I are handed tar-soaked brands. It reminds us of Lewes Bonfire Night preparations, but it's not 5th November and we're not in Lewes.

We are given our destinations. We synchronise our watches, and one by one groups of four or five people leave the house clutching their brands. Our team have been told to go to Thundersbarrow. The other six groups make their way towards other hilltops: Chanctonbury and Wolstonbury hills, Cissbury Ring, Devil's Dyke, Mount Caburn and Hollingbury Camp.

A short drive later it's cold and damp as we walk along the footpath that leads from the car park to this site of an ancient barrow whose name suggests a connection with that old god of thunder: Thor. There's something primal about walking in silence along a track. The person leading the party will be the first to confront any oncoming danger. They are the pioneer leading the way. The one at the back has only darkness behind them. Nobody's got their back and they can be picked off by enemies if that's their fate: by brigands, goblins, ghosts – whoever they might be.

Steph and I are safe in the middle, and soon we're up on the summit of the hill. We look around: dark shapes of the hills in the surrounding landscape, moon and stars out in the sky, a few clouds, ribbons of roads and traffic here and there. We turn towards each other, form a circle and hold hands, tuning in to this land of Sussex beneath us; this soggy grass, this chalk, these sweeping hills with the sea not far away. We remember why we're here: to activate a magical network of energy and light – perhaps just in our imaginations, perhaps in the subtle energy field of the Earth herself, perhaps between groups of ancestors, standing guard in ghostly form over their former habitations: their hillforts, their burial mounds, their look-out points. We begin chanting words of power, as spells are known in magical circles, and then – our intent stated – we turn outward to the hills around us.

One of us spots a sign – a tiny point of waving light over at Hollingbury Camp – and we realise it is one of the other teams waving the light on their phone back and forth to attract our attention. Waving with light – just for fun, just to say hello and 'look what we can do!'

We wait. Fifteen minutes later and it's time. We light our brands, lifting them above our heads and chanting the spell as we gaze out into the darkness. And then, one by one, we see the clusters of torchlight appearing far away – six stars in this constellation we have just created, and our cluster is the seventh and central point of this hexagram. What's going on? What are we doing? My rational mind is sceptical. But my belly, heart and spirit know what's going on: we're linking fire with fire and light with light; networking; connecting; making patterns; weaving the ancient with the Now. Connecting us with the ancestors. It's magic – that's what it is.

There's the everyday, the traffic, the drizzle and the grind, but there's also the unique, the surprising, the moments when we glimpse something beyond the everyday and it feels so worthwhile to be alive. If I've learnt anything – it's that magic can be made.

And then, a year later, I'm sitting in a talk for the Sussex Archaeology Group in Lewes Town Hall, and the speaker, Professor Andy Stirling, makes an extraordinary suggestion about another part of Sussex: that the hills around Lewes might have been seen in ancient times as a sacred landscape that mirrored the pattern of the star cluster of the Pleiades. He points to the ubiquity of stories about the seven visible stars in this cluster, often depicted as seven sisters. We find this motif that has been described as the world's oldest story across all six inhabited continents, including in traditional cultures in Australia, India, Japan, Indonesia, Canada, the USA, Egypt, New Zealand, Greece, Ukraine, Guatemala and Mexico. At Lascaux in France, the Pleiades feature in some of the world's oldest cave art, and the Pleiades are also found represented on the German Late Neolithic Nebra sky disc: the earliest known representation of a star formation on a European artefact. Stirling, keen to avoid the pitfalls of pseudo-history, looked at Ordnance Survey data to find the seven highest points in the Lewes Downs. To his surprise, the seven hill crests obtained from this objective source laid themselves out in a similar pattern to that of the Pleiades. Within this particular landscape, that isn't far from the chalk hill figure of the Long Man, twenty tumuli can be found near these crests, with many more recorded which have since vanished. This evidence of a sacred landscape continues down in the valley where Lewes lies, which by one etymology means 'The Place of the Sacred Mounds'. Here were once at least seven artificial flat-topped mounds like Silbury Hill, though only three remain: the Mount by the old abbey grounds, Brack Mount behind the Lewes Arms, and the mound beneath Lewes Castle.

Perhaps lighting seven brands on seven hilltops at the winter solstice hadn't been such a mad idea after all. On that dark night, the spectacle they created was an imitation of the night sky with seven stars ablaze, and perhaps our ancestors loved to signal to the heavens that we too could radiate constellations of light in the darkness.

And as regards Lewes, why would one town in Sussex end up being unique in the country for having so many artificial mounds, while beside it, on the Downs, a succession of hilltops, home to dozens of tumuli, might have been used as some sort of ritual landscape that mirrored the seven sisters of the Pleiades?

Perhaps only the existence of those mysterious, and contested, ley lines can provide the answer. Alfred Watkins, a surveyor in Herefordshire, came up with the idea, suggesting that in ancient times a system of navigation was developed – a primitive GPS – using landmarks like hilltops, lone trees or copses, tumuli and standing stones with the tracks connecting them being called leys. He suggested that the Long Man of Wilmington is surveying these ley lines – using his staves as markers.

Justin Hopper in *The Old Weird Albion* (2017) writes: 'Lewes is, of course, the centre of Sussex eccentricity. It sits, I will posit, on a convulsion of ley lines: Among too many to name, one that runs from London to Boston, Mass., on which Tom Paine floated into history in the 18th century; one that follows Hilaire Belloc across the Sussex landscape, from pub to pub, venturing in and out of poetry and sobriety; one that traverses the whole of the surface of the earth, in the path of the sun over the planet, from its stage debut each morning as it creeps over Mount Caburn …'

My grandfather, who lived in Hassocks, was a founder member of Watkins' Old Straight Track Club. Club members would go 'ley-hunting' at weekends, sharing notes, trying to build a map of the whole country's ley system. In the club's journal in 1938 he wrote:

'It is a most intriguing and fascinating hobby. In these days when rambling over hill and dale is such a popular amusement, there should be countless opportunities for young people to discover markstones and other reminders of bye-gone days, and to trace out possible alignments from them on the maps when they return home.'

It wasn't until 1969 that one of the founding fathers of the Earth Mysteries movement, John Michell, in his book: *The View Over Atlantis*, suggested that ley lines might be the result of mysterious energies that snake through the Earth, like the dragon lines of China, or the meridians in the human body.

The critique of ley line theory is that Britain is so filled with ancient monuments, churches and hilltops that you can easily trace connections between sites; but if the idea excites you then Sussex is the perfect place to go ley-hunting. Or you may prefer the approach Justin Hopper uses, whereby the leys become tracks in our minds linking the worlds of nature and culture, of past and present, even of fact and speculation, in chains of association, perhaps to inspire, perhaps simply to amaze or entertain. Who knows if Sussex is indeed criss-crossed with 'lines of power' linking one sacred site to another; if Lewes is a great nexus of these lines; if that is why the story arose that the Church of the Holy Sepulchre in Lewes, built by the Knights Templar in 1237 and now the old bus depot, once sheltered the Holy Grail?

As if all these old stories and traces of the past in the landscape aren't enough, it's important to remember that 'sacred' isn't synonymous with 'ancient'. As some of the places you'll discover in this book will reveal, sacred places can be created by us now and in the future.

All these possibilities can make our heads spin. The best cure? Walking the old tracks, letting them speak to us. Here in this book, we share nine walks that will take you to many of the sacred places we've discovered in this county, and by using the Gazetteer you will be able to create your own adventures and pilgrimages. And the exciting thing is that this guide is by no means comprehensive. What we hope is that by following the trails we've suggested, by visiting the sites mentioned, you will be inspired to track down even more magic and mystery.

PART ONE

A GAZETTEER OF SACRED SITES IN SUSSEX

CHALK GODS

ADAM & EVE – THE LONE MAN & THE WHITE HORSE

The Downland of Sussex appears deceptively straightforward: great sweeps of gentle hills often denuded by millennia of sheep farming, which began here in 3000 BCE. But go to the edges of the Downs as they fall – sometimes literally – into the sea, at a place like Seven Sisters, and you get a glimpse of the hidden power that lies here. The father of the English Druid revival in the 17th century, John Aubrey, said of this landscape: 'They are the most spacious plains in Europe, and the greatest remains that I can hear of the smooth primitive world when it lay all under water.' The occult writer Dion Fortune (1890–1946) said that the chalk Downs were the best place to evoke the old gods, for they are the primeval landscape of southern England and have been admired and written about by countless Englishmen and foreigners. And what better way to evoke and honour the old gods and goddesses than to imprint one of them into the landscape?

The Long Man

Alongside Sussex's Seven Sisters, the chalk figure of the Wilmington Giant has to be the county's most iconic image. And like all good things it is shrouded in mystery. The Long Man, The Lone Man, The Lanky Man, The Green Man (all have been local names for him) is both enchanting and vast. At 227 feet (70 metres) tall he is the largest representation of a human figure in Europe and in the world second only to the Giant of Atacama in northern Chile, who stands 393 feet (119 metres) tall.

The Wilmington Giant was, up to 150 years ago, actually a green man. If he ever was originally a classic chalk hill figure cut into the turf, then the periodical scouring needed to stop the grass encroaching on his outline must have been abandoned many centuries previously and as a result he was a god who appeared on the hillside only under certain conditions. Until the 19th century he was often known as the Green Man of Wilmington. Covered in grass, the Green God would appear only at early morning or late evening on certain days when there was sufficient sun at the right angle. After it had snowed, he would appear briefly as the snow thawed, since the snow stayed a little longer in the shallow recesses of his outline than on the surrounding grass.

When the green giant became the white giant in a restoration of chalk bricks, led by the vicar of Glynde in 1874, an error was made in the outline of one foot: writings and photographs taken before the bricking indicate that the giant originally had both feet pointing down the slope – as if he was skiing down the hillside or standing on tiptoe. But now one foot was made to turn to the left – making the figure look as if it belongs to an Egyptian frieze.

The figure's location is very particular. Drawn in a natural amphitheatre of the Downs, from many angles he is obscured from view. Walking the South Downs Way over Windover Hill, you do not see him. It is only when he is approached from the north that you come upon him, as if this chalk giant is a mysterious guardian or protector of this range of the South Downs. For the dark half of the year, from Samhain (end of October), he remains in darkness, until at Beltane, at the beginning of May, the sunlight can finally reach him.

Many have speculated about a connection between the Cerne Abbas Giant in Dorset and the Long Man. The former stands 180 feet (55 metres) high and brandishes an oak leaf-shaped club in his right hand. That he is a symbol of rampant male fertility is in little doubt;

it was once a common practice for barren women to sit on his 30-foot (9-metre) long erection in the hope of a cure. The Long Man, by contrast, evokes an entirely different response from the viewer. Alfred Watkins believed that he was a 'dodman': a prehistoric surveyor, carrying the two sighting rods he needed to develop or survey the old straight track system of ley lines. A more satisfying theory is that he stands at a threshold, guarding the doorway not just to the South Downs but to the Underworld or Otherworld. Here, perhaps, we see him as he truly is – a giant, a god, who comes from the south, the place of the maximum heat and light of the sun, and who faces the north, the place of the goddess and darkness. He stands holding open the gates of Time – the gates to the Underworld – but also bars our way to that secret place within the hills.

The Long Man's lack of a rather important appendage may, at one level, have a simple explanation: the removal of phalluses by god-fearing archaeologists, town councillors, clergy and workmen was once common practice in less enlightened times. The clue as to when it may well have disappeared comes from the account of Dr. J.S. Phené who 'discovered' the Long Man in the 1870s and who initiated the marking out of the giant's outline in yellowish-white bricks at the expense of the Duke of Devonshire, and under the direction of the vicar of Glynde, the Revd de St Croix. He wrote that when he visited the Cerne Giant he found that he could only do so by 'overcoming with difficulty his repugnance at inspecting that figure'.

One of the figure's most extraordinary attributes is that he has been created with a deliberate distortion that makes him appear normally proportioned when viewed from the surrounding countryside. If you took a plane and flew over him, you would discover that he has been drawn with exactly the right degree of distortion, so that when viewed from the ground this creates the effect of the giant actually standing up, rather than lying on the ground.

Like the Cerne Giant, the actual age of the Long Man remains uncertain. In 2003 archaeological investigations suggested that he may have been created in the 16th or 17th century, leading some to speculate that he was created as a Tudor political satire. It doesn't seem very likely. Or very funny. The Cerne Giant is estimated to have been created any time between 700 CE and 1600 CE. If neither were painstakingly created as a joke – especially considering the hostility and fear around paganism in the Middle Ages – and taking into account too that these figures have been tampered with over the time, we may still keep an open mind to the possibility that Sussex's great giant may be thousands not hundreds of years old. The reality is that any ancient origin for these figures is likely to be lost in the earth. The discovery of remains that can be dated proves only that the figures existed at that time, but it does not – and cannot – prove that there was nothing there before that.

In recent years the Long Man has inspired songs and an oratorio, it has been a backdrop to pop videos, has appeared in Neil Gaiman's *The Sandman* (1988), has given his name to a local brewery and beer, and has inspired others to create their own chalk giants. In 1994, in protest against the Tory government's road-building madness, the cartoonist Steve Bell created a hill figure near Brighton of Prime Minister John Major wearing only underpants, with a traffic cone on his head. Later those naughty St Trinianesque girls of Roedean painted a replica of the Long Man on the school lawn, generously restoring his manhood, and ensuring that helicopters were soon flying overhead to photograph their handiwork for the papers. It cannot have been a coincidence that their history teacher was Rodney Castleden, author of *The Wilmington Giant* (1983). The Long Man has, of course, also been 'hacked' several times. In the third millennium he briefly acquired the words 'FRACK OFF!'; he donned a mask during COVID and was once feminised by TV's Trinny and Susannah with pigtails, breasts and hips.

This leads us to one final area for contemplation: the very notion that the figure is, indeed, a man. Many consider the Wilmington Giant's gender to be ambiguous or perceive 'him' as androgynous, a non-binary 'they'. 'He' could even be a 'she'; those hips might be seen as having child-bearing qualities. Do we need to ascribe a gender to the figure at all? Like the final card in the Major Arcana of the Tarot, the World, which depicts a hermaphrodite, might the Long Man perhaps be a vast message carved in the earth, reminding us of the necessity to unite the opposites? More than we can hope for in our times, the Wilmington Giant may show us the way beyond the particularity and limitations of gender.

And finally, as a place of worship and ritual, the Long Man continues to be used by druids eight times a year on the Sundays that fall closest to the solstices, equinoxes and other ceremonial days that lie on the Druid and Pagan Eightfold Wheel of the Year. After a good afternoon's ritual where better to slake one's thirst than the Long Man Inn in the village itself?

Litlington White Horse

Just 3 miles (4.8 kilometres) from the Long Man lies one of many equine shapes cut into the British landscape. Sussex's own white horse lies between Litlington and West Dean on High-and-Over Hill (Hindover Hill) facing north-east. Measuring 90 feet (27 metres) in height it was created by three local men under moonlight in 1924 – replacing one that had been cut there in the mid-19th century – and renovated in 1949. Like the Wilmington Giant it too has occasionally been hacked, acquiring a rather fetching unicorn's horn in 2017. Nowhere near as large, old, mysterious or impressive as the White Horse at Uffington, it is still a delight to come across in the landscape and is best viewed walking south along the banks of the River Cuckmere from Litlington village. An intriguing wisp of folk memory relates that the two carved images in the land found here and at Wilmington were known by locals as Adam and Eve.

SACRED STONES

SARSENS, THE GOLDSTONE & GURDY STONE

Sussex isn't noted for its megalithic henges, mighty monoliths or dolmens, and for good reason: it doesn't really have any. This is due in part to the geological dominance of flint and chalk; neither make for good monuments. That virtually all the landscape here has been altered through farming and housing is another factor. The presence in the landscape of sarsen stones – the kind found at Stonehenge – do suggest however, that some megaliths did once inhabit the landscape. Many of Sussex's churches have sarsen stones in their grounds or built into the foundations of the churches themselves, evidence that these buildings may have been built directly on sacred pagan sites. But what the county lacks in the old, it makes up for in the new. Ditchling is home to Sussex's only stone circle – built in the private garden of a local farmhouse and decidedly modern – while in 2023 the village of Kingston acquired a new slate monolith which also stands on farmland and was erected with ritual in mind.

The Goldstone

South-west corner of Hove Park, Park View Road, Hove BN3 7BF

If you hadn't gathered by now, the Devil certainly gets around in Sussex. After his attempts to flood the county at Devil's Dyke were thwarted, he stubbed his toe on a particularly large rock while furiously digging and gave it an almighty boot (clearly having not learnt his lesson). The rock sailed over the Downs and landed in what is now known as Goldstone Bottom. During the 19th century tourists, druids and those of a Romantic bent came to seek out this 'Goldstone', Tolmen or Druid Stone, attracted by stories that here had once been a meeting place of the ancient druids. The Goldstone was said to glitter in sunlight, leading some to have once suggested that it might even be a meteorite (it is in fact a combination of flint and sandstone). By 1834, the owner of Goldstone Farm, on which it resided, became so irritated with all the sightseers the stone attracted that he had it buried. Sixty-odd years later – and thanks to the only living person in the area who remembered where it had been buried – the stone was exhumed and placed in the newly opened Hove Park in 1906 where it remains to this day, encircled by six smaller stones. In the early 20th century, Sussex writer Thomas Walker Horsfield described the Goldstone as 'one of the largest and most remarkable of the Druidical stones on the Downs', though the competition is hardly stiff. Standing a little over 6 feet (1.8 metres) and a bit lumpy, the Goldstone is in truth rather unassuming, but if you do visit it's worth looking for 'Rockfeller'. In 1913 local artist Clem Lambert noticed that if the rock is viewed north from Old Shoreham Road on a sunny morning, a craggy face with a bulbous floppy nose might reveal itself to you, looking a bit like Walter Matthau.

Local sources from the 19th and 20th century suggest that a circle of up to twenty stones – of which the Goldstone may have been one – once stood on the Downs, the largest of which were buried; the smaller ones broken up and used to form the base of Victoria Fountain in Brighton at the Steine. Others suggest that the stones in the fountain may have come from a stone circle that once stood at the site of Brighton's oldest church: St Nicholas's. While the exact history may never be uncovered there is little doubt that these stones were brought here for sacred and ritualistic purposes. For a brief period in the 20th century the Goldstone itself became the focal point of modern-day pagan rites. In 1929 an oak tree was planted close by and a ceremony and banquet held and attended by many local druids celebrating the 100th chapter of the Brighton & Hove Royal Arch (Ancient Order of

Druids). The Old Steine fountain in Brighton also became the focus of healing ceremonies and meditations from 1981 via a spiritual group that started in Brighton known as Fountain International. A plaque in their honour can be found to the north of the fountain.

The Gurdy Stone *lovebrook.org*
Lovebrook Farm, The Street, Kingston, Near Lewes BN7 3NT
Open: *Saturdays only dawn–1pm*

While Victorian farmers and landowners were in the habit of breaking up and burying sacred stones (Avebury in Wiltshire suffered a similar fate in the 19th century), one modern-day farm – in Sussex at least – has welcomed a new monolith on its land. It's not often you get to witness the arrival of a new sacred stone but on Saturday 22nd April 2023 musical duo Local Psycho – Jem Finer and Jimmy Cauty best known as one half of the KLF – gathered forty-odd people in the centre of a field in Kingston for the erection of a 2½-tonne Welsh slate monolith named the Gurdy Stone. Here it is hoped to remain for the next 50,000 years, enough time, as decreed by its creators, to herald in the return of the Green Comet.

The Gurdy Stone originally came from a quarry in Wales and on the day of its erection was carried to its chosen location by a digger while the invited throng swayed in time to the music, rather like the residents of Summerisle preparing for their blood sacrifice of poor Sergeant Howie in the cult film *The Wicker Man*. Once the stone was in place, a spiral was laid out around it and those gathered were invited to participate in a ritual to walk the spiral and place a small stone at the foot of the monolith. A week later the Gurdy Stone was again the focal point of an all-day pagan-friendly event known as Pillars of Wisdom. For now, it patiently awaits the return of the comet and can be viewed on the left in its field if walking up The Street in Kingston from the main road or visited between dawn and 1pm every Saturday.

The Steyning Stone
This can be found in the entrance to St Andrew and St Cuthman's Church (see a description of the stone in Walk 8 on page 86).

HOLY WATERS

CHALK RIVERS, SACRED WELLS & SPRINGS

Most of the chalk rivers in Europe are to be found in England, and in Sussex there are three of these: the Ems and Lavant in West Sussex and the Lewes Winterbourne in East Sussex. There are also over 87 miles (140 kilometres) of chalk streams threading their way through the South Downs National Park and the Chichester Coastal Plain, and the gradient of these streams is much steeper than those of the rivers, resulting in specific habitats for a range of plants, including the magnificently named blunt-fruited water-starwort and lesser water-parsnip.

Since these chalk rivers and streams are fed from groundwater aquifers, particularly clean, clear water flows along them at relatively stable water temperatures. Whether from these sources or from the chalybeate (containing salts of iron) springs found in Tunbridge Wells and Hastings, found in the walks on pages 69–72 and 78–82, we know that both our Christian and pre-Christian ancestors revered and prized clean life-giving water in a way that we can emulate today, and that puts our national water agencies to shame.

A number of holy wells and springs existed in Sussex that sadly no longer exist, including in Shoreham, Winchelsea and Battle. Some village pumps may have begun life as sacred wells and can be seen in locations like Willingdon and Stanmer village. Two wells that can still be visited are described opposite.

Fulking Spring

The Street (nr The Shepherd & Dog pub), Fulking, West Sussex BN5 9LU

Reformer John Ruskin (1819–1900) enjoyed visiting Sussex over the mid-to-late 19th century, and was particularly fond of the pretty village of Fulking whose natural spring was a popular spot for sheep washing. Ruskin clearly charmed the locals with his knowledge and wisdom as they sought his advice on how to harness the local water. What advice he offered is not recorded but it obviously hit the mark as in 1886 a ceramic tiled fountain was erected in his honour. On it is written: 'To the glory of God and in honour of John Ruskin' followed by 'Psalm LXXVIII: That they might see their hope in God and not forget but keep his Commandments who brought streams also out of the Rock.'

Holywell Eastbourne

At the western end of the Eastbourne promenade you will find the Italian Gardens: a charming dell-like area of lawns and flower beds, a tea room and beach chalets. It's also known as the Holywell Retreat. Opinions as to the origin of this name vary: some refer to the local pronunciation – 'Holly Well' – which suggests there was a spring by a holly tree. Others think it could indicate the location of a spring used by a holy man. Whatever its true origin, it was known about over 300 years ago. James Royer's 1787 guide to Eastbourne states that 'one of the springs is called Holy-well, supposed to be so named from the many advantages received from drinking those waters.'

It is likely that the well still exists, and can be found about 437 yards (400 metres) to the west of the Italian Gardens at the base of the cliffs. Towering above the cliff known as 'Gibraltar', rain water filters down through the chalk and emerges through the rocks. In 2009 the spring was discovered or re-discovered and a sign erected, with the local Catholic church conducting two blessings there in subsequent years.

The Lost Spring of St Helen's Woods

See Walk 7 on page 78.

MAGICAL TREES

A GILDED ELM, ANCIENT YEWS & GNARLED OAKS

Trees are as integral to a sacred landscape as hills and standing stones, churches and holy wells. As living beings they stand as guardians of the land around them, and it is no wonder that they were revered by our ancestors and associated with powers of healing and protection. The ancient druids, whom the classical writers tell us originated in mainland Britain, placed the tree at the heart of their worship. The Roman historian Tacitus wrote: 'The grove is the centre of their whole religion.' Traces of druid treelore, the Celtic tree wisdom of Ogham, folklore and local customs all combine to offer a rich harvest to anyone seeking to deepen their connection to trees as evocative sources of poetic and spiritual inspiration.

The Yew

The yew is a tree that invites veneration – its dark shade and often gnarled form can evoke fear, but also wonder. In ancient times, yew woods like the surviving Kingley Vale in West Sussex were undoubtedly more common, and archaeologists have unearthed the traces of yew woodland in places like Mount Caburn near Lewes. Ioho – in Irish – is the tree of death and rebirth, a sacred tree of the druids. Recently it has been found that yews can live for at least 3,000 years. This fact, combined with it being an evergreen, points to it as the tree of eternal life. Yet in the popular imagination it is a tree of death –

partly because its leaves are poisonous (its Latin genus name *Taxus* may be the origin of our word toxic) but mainly because it grows in churchyards. The mundane explanation for the favouring of yews near graves is that it kept animals out of the churchyards – both they and their owners knew of their danger. The esoteric explanation is that it represents the survival of a pagan knowledge that the yew was the tree of rebirth and eternal life, and that it was therefore most fitting as a graveyard tree. In the druid tree-calendar, Ioho is placed at the time of Samhain (pronounced 'Sow-in'). Samhain, in the three days between 31st October and 2nd November, represents the time of death and the potential for rebirth. At this time druids honour the ancestors, the departed ones, and prepare for a new cycle of the year. Later these three days were Christianised and became Hallowe'en, All Saints' Day and All Souls' Day.

For the most awe-inspiring experience of yews, visit the Kingley Vale Yew Forest (see Walk 2 on page 59). The Wilmington Yew (described in Walk 6 on page 73) is at least 1,600 years old and is also worth a dedicated visit – especially since it is so close to the Long Man of Wilmington and a fine pub – the Long Man Inn. The Crowhurst Yew, in the churchyard of St George's Church, Crowhurst, just outside Hastings, is also a fitting pilgrimage destination. Although often referred to as 'the oldest tree in Sussex', it is probably younger than the Wilmington Yew – but it is still impressive enough to awaken those ancestral urges to actually worship these magnificent beings. The Coldwaltham Yew in the churchyard of St Giles' Church in Coldwaltham, near Pulborough, is also majestic, over 34 feet (10 metres) in height and completely hollow, with enough room to fit two people standing. It seems that this yew was once a site of folk magic: many nails have been found driven into it, suggesting an apotropaic ritual designed to ward off evil.

The Elm

In Celtic mythology the elm, like the yew, is also associated with death and transformation. Our once-common native tree was favoured by travelling preachers, under which they would hold sermons, and also – according to legend – by elves, who guarded the underworld entrances found near mighty elms. The elm's association with death even extended to the traditional use of its wood for making coffins. This, of course was before the dreaded Dutch Elm Disease, which has made the existence of mature elm trees in Britain now such a rarity.

The Gilded Elm

South-west corner of Preston Park, Brighton

Brighton residents may not be aware but their city has more varieties of elm that any other in the world. It has also done more than most in fighting off Dutch Elm Disease. Lost in 2019, however, was one of Preston Park's twin elms, first planted in 1613 when Brighton was just a fishing village, making them the joint oldest elm trees in the world. After being ravaged by elm bark beetles, one of the elms had to be chopped down but was reunited with its twin in 2020 by artist Elpida Hadzi-Vasileva who removed the bark, coated the remains in black oils, strengthened the insides and gilded parts of the remaining 6½ feet (2 metres) of the truncated tree. Now this beautiful work of art may be the first elm tree to not only symbolise death and rebirth but one that has gone through its own alchemical transmutation into gold.

The Oak

Druids revere all trees, but oaks and yews are held in particular esteem. The oak represents stability, tradition and connection to deity, with the word druid meaning 'oak sage' or 'oak seer'. Sussex has some splendid oaks, which include:

At Crowhurst, just five minutes from the station, in front of St George's Church, you'll find an enormous majestic oak growing on the bank in front of the church. Just beyond this guardian tree you can visit the Crowhurst Yew.

In Cowdray Park near Lodsworth in West Sussex, you can see one of the oldest oaks in Britain. The Queen Elizabeth Oak – so-called because Queen Elizabeth I was said to have sheltered within it in 1591 – is between 800 and 1,000 years old, and has been designated one of fifty Great British Trees by the Tree Council. Low in height but with a vast girth, an entire coven or congregation could now fit inside its hollow trunk.

In Petworth Park you can follow the National Trust's Ancient Tree Walk which takes you past wonderful specimens of ancient oak, including the Norman Oak that dates back to the Norman Conquest.

At Chidham Peninsula in Chichester Harbour, not only can you see wonderful views of the coast in this designated Area of Outstanding Natural Beauty, but you can also experience the eerie sight of wind-blown gnarled oaks, their growth stunted by sea salt, their boughs reaching out towards the sea.

PILGRIM PATHS

HIGHWAYS, ANCIENT TRACKS & PILGRIM ROUTES

Anglo-French writer and historian Hilaire Belloc (1870–1953) said that the road represented 'the greatest and the most original of the spells which we inherit from the earliest pioneers of our race'. Just as fire evokes within us the appreciation of spirit, and we feel drawn to a fireside as if by an implacable spell, so too does an ancient trackway evoke in us the spirit of journeying and the experience of both freedom and belonging to the earth.

In southern England in Neolithic times, trackways began to be permanently engraved on the landscape, although the dramatic changes in climate, vegetation, and animal and human populations would have led to much erasure and change. Some of these trackways were originally made by animals and were then followed by us. Others became major routes and the term 'highway' comes precisely from one particular kind of trackway that is distinctive in England: the highways, the ancient tracks that follow the ridges of high land.

Plotting these ancient tracks on a map immediately shows us why the great sites of Silbury Hill, Avebury and Stonehenge were positioned where they were: for they lie, broadly speaking, at the point of convergence of five great trackways. The South Downs Way is one such 'highway'.

The idea of pilgrimage became a popular means of connecting with faith in the Middle Ages and while most pilgrim paths in Western

Europe are Christian, nowadays they are used by anyone seeking a connection with spirituality, with nature, to improve their well-being, or when faced with a crossroads or crisis.

Along with such popular routes as the Wealdway, Greenwich Meridian Trail, Sussex Diamond Way and the Sussex Border Path, Britain's most popular pilgrim route, the Old Way, meanders through Sussex, starting at Winchester and finishing in Canterbury, Kent. The more recently designed Cuckmere Pilgrim Path takes a beautiful 12-mile (19-kilometre) circular route around the Cuckmere Valley taking in seven key churches and villages. And while the Ouse Valley Way is not a traditional pilgrim route, water has long been worshipped and associated with healing and transformation.

The South Downs Way

The most well-known ancient highway in Sussex is the South Downs Way – a 100-mile (160-kilometre) long drover's path that is thought to be at least 8,000 years old. Certainly our Neolithic ancestors would have traversed these hills regularly – their forts and burial mounds can be found all the way along it. Officially opened as a National Trail in 1972 the South Downs Way initially ran the entirety of Sussex from Buriton on the West Sussex border to Eastbourne, but was later extended to Winchester. It incorporates much that is sacred in the county's landscapes including Chanctonbury Ring, Devil's Dyke and the Long Man.

Walked as a sacred path from west to east you might like to start at Winchester Cathedral by lighting a candle and saying a prayer for the journey ahead, or perhaps a simple ritual at the foot of the Downs, pertinent to some kind of transformation or resolution you're seeking to achieve on your journey ahead. Regardless of the time of year, those sensitive to the airier elements will find that earplugs are your friend; the wind can really whip around you on these hills. With the path ending in Eastbourne it seems only right that such a journey should end by contemplating the sacredness of life, mortality and where to get the best fish and chips.

The Sussex Ouse Valley Way: Lower Beeding to the sea

If ever there was a way to soothe the soul, it is to spend time sitting by or walking along a river. This 42-mile (68-kilometre) waterside walk follows Sussex's River Ouse (or travels close to it when there is no public right of way) from its source near Lower Beeding all the way to Seaford Bay. Flat, gentle and meandering, the path weaves its way through Barcombe Mills, Lewes, Southease and Piddinghoe before finally reaching the sea. Symbolically, rivers can serve as boundaries, the crossing of which transform us from one stage of life to another, including death. They can also symbolise wisdom, growth and new beginnings. This was certainly the case for Sussex author Olivia Laing who set out to walk the Ouse Valley Way in 2011 after the end of a job and a relationship break-up left her feeling displaced. Writing about it in her book *To the River*, Laing ruminates on the roles that she sees rivers playing in our own lives, well-being and mythology. For her, the walk along the Ouse was cathartic and cleansing. For those times in life when things get overwhelming, this pilgrimage might just be the ticket.

The Cuckmere Pilgrim Path
See Walk 6 on page 73.

ANCIENT SETTLEMENTS

FROM GOOSEHILL CAMP
TO HASTINGS CASTLE

An impressive array of Bronze and Iron Age hillforts once peppered the tops of the Downs, across East and West Sussex and beyond. While most are lost to us now through farming, housing and land management, the earthworks – bank and ditches – of some of those ancient settlements remain embedded in the landscape, reminding us that for thousands of years we have been sculpting and transforming the Sussex terrain for our own needs.

The remains of huts, pottery, weapons, bones, bronze daggers, metal and flint tools have all been found at these sites – giving clues as to certain aspects of how our ancestors might have lived. Some have suggested that they were settlements with huts for homes and places for trades and craft. Yet many show little or no evidence of human habitation. Would it make sense to live on an exposed windy hill, miles from a water source and with all good agricultural land down below? Others believe that the earthworks and ramparts were built purely for military protection in case of invasion and for protection and storage of such produce as grain. Too often, however, we forget to consider the spiritual and psychological values of our ancient ancestors. Like indigenous and animist cultures around the globe, wouldn't the lives of our ancestors have been rich with ritual, ceremony, nature-worship and magic?

Around twenty-five hillforts across Sussex are known to us, from Goosehill Camp, Highdown Hill and Chanctonbury Ring in the west to Hollingbury and Hastings Castle in the east. One of them, Harrow Hill, may take its name from *hearg*, a Saxon word for hilltop heathen shrine. Ritual deposits found at many of these sites strongly suggest that hillforts weren't simply for defences against potential aggressors but for votive offerings too. That our hillforts also served a sacred purpose is looking increasingly likely; the nature of the rituals and beliefs of their creators, however, may always remain a mystery.

Hollingbury Camp
Ditchling Road. Accessed via Hollingbury Golf Course, Brighton BN1 7HS

That the neighbourhood of Hollingbury on the outskirts of Brighton may have derived its name from Holy Buri – a sacred mount – is not altogether unlikely; it is, after all, home to an impressive 4,000-year-old Bronze Age hillfort, overlooked by most owing to its location in the centre of a popular golf course. But it may be this very fact that saved Hollingbury from a similar fate to that of Whitehawk Camp just a few miles away: being subsumed by a race course and housing estate.

Hollingbury Camp was excavated twice in the 20th century, revealing entrances at the east and west of the hill, evidence of several huts – 20–40 feet (6–12 metres) in length – and four mounds, the highest of which is thought to have once supported a beacon. The presence of oak trees in nearby ancient woods has led some to speculate that this camp may once have been a site of druidic activity; oaks do not normally grow on chalk escarpments, but were of course favoured for druidic groves.

To find the hillfort, head up the long hill of Ditchling Road until you reach the golf course. Two public paths on your right, at either end of the golf course, lead across the course into woodland. Follow directions on public information signs and you'll eventually find the camp. That it is somewhat hidden away makes for a more enchanting experience, though it pays to be wary of golf balls on your way out and in, and is best visited at dawn on a golden summer's morning.

A clear chalk path circumambulates the top of the fort with spectacular views of the Downs, Brighton, Lewes and its chalk cliffs and, of course, the sea. In spring and summer daisies and buttercups grow amongst the gorse and grasses, and the air is filled with the sounds of skylarks. In the centre of the camp four paths cross and the gorse thickens. Here you and the natural world can feel secluded from busy Brighton and modern life as if the camp's past is encroaching on the present. It can be a perfect spot for morning meditation or at midnight when the veil between this world and the next is thin. But wait! Was it your imagination or did four robed figures just pass through the bushes sporting headdresses, staffs and amulets?

Chanctonbury Ring Hillfort
See Walk 8, page 83.

Cissbury Ring Hillfort
See Walk 1, page 56.

Mount Caburn Hillfort
See Walk 9, page 88.

BARROWS, TUMULI & TUMPS

THE LEWES TUMP
& THE DEVIL'S JUMPS

What Sussex lacks in stone circles and monoliths it more than makes up for in its tumuli, tumps, hillforts and Neolithic monuments. In fact, some of Britain's oldest markers of Neolithic life can be found here. First and foremost, however, it's probably wise to define our terms.

Tumuli or barrows are Bronze Age burial mounds, perhaps used as initiation chambers or megalithic sweat lodges – places of darkness, of death-and-rebirth, of sensory deprivation, vision questing, isolation and of communion with the ancestors. They are of the long or round variety, usually indicating a communal burial place in the long form, an individual one in the rounded. The key place in a tumulus is within. The power exists within its womb-chamber. They are important and powerful features of our Sussex landscape: at least nineteen in the Lewes area alone have been recorded. A number of the churches in Sussex were built either next to or directly onto these barrows.

Sacred mounds – sometimes called tumps, mumps, mounts or toots – are almost certainly human-made artificial conical hills, often with quite steep sides and flat tops, and clearly built with a very different purpose and character to barrows and tumuli, but one that we can only surmise from our viewpoint thousands of years later. You can't enter one physically because you are not supposed to – there is no chamber or passageway to its heart. The place of power is atop. The most famous of them all is Silbury in Avebury, Wiltshire. For centuries Silbury Hill was believed to be the resting place of a chieftain or a long forgotten 'King Sil', with myriad treasures that were said to be buried along with his body. Despite an excavation of Silbury Hill during Victorian times yielding little, the tump was excavated again in 1969 and part of it broadcast as live TV. Again, the results were initially disappointing – no burial chamber was found, no chieftain or king accompanied by grave goods was disturbed by the archaeologists. What they did discover was far more exciting. Deep inside the great mound they found a small conical hill. Under this was found a radial pattern of ropes. The organic matter excavated from beneath the mound gave a radiocarbon date of around 2150 BCE. The remains of vegetation and trapped insects even suggested a particular time of year that the mound was raised – the last week of July or the first week of August. Midway between these two weeks lies the time of Lughnasadh, the harvest festival later Christianised as Lammastide or Lammas. In Scotland up until the 18th century, Lammas towers were built to celebrate this festival. Conical mounds about 8 feet (2.5 metres) high would be built of turves and each community would build a tower in a conspicuous place, which served as a focal point for the Lammas celebrations. The information obtained from the Silbury Hill excavation suggests it may have been a hill built for Lughnasadh celebrations – a giant harvest hill created by probably hundreds of people. Another reason why this is of great interest to us is that Lewes may contain one too.

Lewes Tump

While Wiltshire's Silbury Hill remains the most well-known mound or tump, there are a remarkable number in Sussex. Yet only Lewes boasts one that is such a large, distinct feature of the landscape. Despite being located close to Lewes Priory, few people pay any attention to it. It is popularly believed to be made up of the rubble excavated from the old salt flats – now called the Dripping Pan. Others believe it is a Calvary Hill constructed by the monks at the Priory – and hence its use today to raise a cross at Easter. In *The Wilmington Giant* (1983), the historian Rodney Castleden suggests the mound was built as a form of prehistoric solar observatory, as Stonehenge seems to be, since at this place the hills on the horizon are sufficiently close to provide orientations to the midwinter and midsummer sunrises and sunsets even in poor visibility. Five thousand years ago, standing here on this mound, you would have seen the midsummer sun rise precisely over Cliffe Hill round barrow only three quarters of a mile away. At sunset you would have seen the sunset over the Blackcap barrows just 3 miles distant. At midwinter, you would have seen the rebirth of the sun directly above the Beddingham Hill barrow, 3½ miles away, and its setting over Swanborough Hill barrow, 2½ miles away. By positioning barrows and the Lewes Mount in this way, Castleden suggested they created a sun-clock, a green clock-face of the Green King, as he has called it.

The similarities between Lewes Tump and Silbury Hill are striking. Both are artificial hills, both are made of chalk, both are turf-covered, both are conical with the apex of the cone absent, both have a circular platform at the summit, both have slopes at around 30 degrees, both have ledges or ways below the summit and both have valley-floor sites with nearby wetlands. One theory on the etymology of Lewes is that it comes from the Saxon *Hlaewes* (The Place of the Mounds), and at least seven mounds were once here in this town. Three remain, the Tump and one at the castle, the other (Brack Mount) behind the Lewes Arms, and both were used as mottes. No-one is sure whether they were constructed from ground level up, but it is quite possible that already existing mounds or barrows were simply increased in size, since the castles at Chichester and Canterbury, founded at the same time as Lewes, seem to have been built on Roman tumuli.

The other mounds have been demolished but are referred to in parish records. One was at the site of the Elephant & Castle pub and one at the site of Abinger House – an immense tumulus was removed for a Mr Barratt to build his home. At St John sub Castro two mounds were levelled here: one of these was called St John's Mount and was recorded by Gideon Mantell (1790–1852) of dinosaur fame, who said skeletons, and a large quantity of boars' and other animal bones were found. He suggested it was a site for 'Druidical sepulchres'.

The fact that at least seven mounds were built in Lewes, suggests it was a place of special spiritual significance. And since the archaeological evidence strongly suggests that Silbury was built as a giant harvest hill, it is possible that in Lewes too our ancestors would have climbed in celebration the snake-path towards the summit of the Tump. There they would have looked down at the ripe fields and up at the sun blessing their land.

There is, however, a spanner (or spade) in the works for this theory. Radiocarbon dating by an archaeological team in 2016 suggests the Tump is no older than the 16th or 17th century, and was built after the Priory's dissolution. This led the team to conjecture that it may have been a 'garden feature' of the manor house that was built here after the Reformation. In Wiltshire, however, known megalithic tumps were converted into garden mounds around the same time, so can we be entirely certain about the origin of this mound?

Whether it was built from scratch as a 'Prospect Hill' four or five hundred years ago for rich people to survey the countryside, or whether it began life much earlier as a harvest mound, today it is the focus for religious and magical devotions. At Easter a cross is raised on the Tump after a parade in town, and every so often druids and pagans celebrate one of the solstices or equinoxes or cross-quarter days here.

Since the site is minutes away from Lewes station, is next to a car park, and the town is filled with eateries, the Tump makes a perfect place to start or end a pilgrimage or magical walk. After clarifying your intentions for the walk, and beginning perhaps with a wish or prayer for a fruitful adventure, you might like to set off for Mount Caburn, to then take the train from Glynde back to Lewes, or to walk in any number of directions. For more information on the Tump and on sacred Sussex, see *The Druid Way* (1993) by Philip Carr-Gomm.

Adsdean Down Tumuli

Kingley Vale, West Sussex

Close to Kingley Vale and its majestic Devil's Humps is a Neolithic feature unique to the whole of the UK: a twin-belled barrow, a pair of conjoined barrows which look, as archaeologist Dom Escott writes in *Ancestors of Adsdean Down*, 'like a single living cell about to divide into two'.

These tumuli are surrounded by a ditch with a smaller bowl barrow located nearby that some have suggested imply a family burial, and while partially covered in brambles are fairly well preserved.

They can be found by heading west out of Stoughton, down the Adsdean Park Road and following a clear pathway east through woodland, passing the tumuli after less than a mile.

Devil's Jumps
Near Treyford, West Sussex
Follow a footpath nr the Royal Oak at Hooksway

Proof that, despite the traffic on the A27, the Devil really does get around the county, local legend has it that near Treyford in West Sussex the horned one used to keep himself endlessly amused by hopping and leaping from the landscape's manmade hillocks. Trouble was, this didn't amuse the hammer-wielding stormy-tempered Thor who liked to sit up here and eat his sandwiches on a warm afternoon. Enraged at seeing the Devil on his turf, Thor lobbed a rock at him and he scarpered. And while the Devil never returned, he did give his name to the feature which doubtless played havoc with Thor's fragile ego too. The Devil's Jumps – not to be confused with the Devil's Humps at Kingley Vale – are five bell barrows in total, each with a circular ditch and thought to be 3,000–4,000 years old. Probably the best-preserved of their kind in the county, they run north-west to south-east propounding the theory that they have been deliberately aligned to the sunset on midsummer's day.

They can be seen on the South Downs Way between Treyford and North Marsden, north of Chichester.

Devil's Humps
Kingley Vale, West Sussex
See Walk 2, page 59.

SACRED BUILDINGS, HOMES & COMMUNITIES

CHURCHES, A MONASTERY & A QUEER PLACE

Nowadays we mostly visit sacred sites as tourists, pilgrims or spiritual seekers, but the sites themselves evolved as places used and lived in by the local community. Here they built homes and churches, communities and monasteries. Inspired to join them, some of these places have attracted residents from across the world: Subud members to Lewes, radical Christians to the German Bruderhof community in Darvell, followers of Rudolf Steiner's teachings to Forest Row and East Grinstead.

Chithurst Buddhist Monastery cittaviveka.org
Chithurst, West Sussex GU31 5EU
Open: April–December

Chithurst Monastery a.k.a Cittaviveka is a serene and beautiful retreat set in 173 acres (70 hectares) of woodland and meadows in deepest West Sussex. It makes for an idyllic spot to recharge the proverbial batteries or to spend some quiet contemplative hours or even days. The monks and nuns who live here are part of an order known as the Forest Tradition which grew out of Thailand at the beginning of the 20th century while still very much being affiliated with one of the oldest extant Buddhist schools, Theravada. The monastery was established in 1979 after the order acquired Hammer Wood in West Sussex and the then dilapidated Chithurst House, less than a mile apart. Over the decades various buildings have sprung up in the grounds, including workshops, residential houses and huts, and the stunning Dhamma Hall with its cloisters, quad, pond and a large sunny meditation room.

The monastery is open to visitors from April to December inclusive. When entering the main buildings, you'll be expected to remove your shoes, so it's best not wear knee-high Dr Martens for your visit. If you'd like to eat here you'll need to arrive at 10.30am in summer and 11.30am in winter (but do check the website beforehand). Buffet-type vegan and vegetarian food is served to monks, residential guests and visitors alike at this time via the kitchen in the main house. It's good etiquette however to allow a little time for residents to get their food first. When warm, the back garden of the house is a beautiful spot in which to eat or sit in silent contemplation overlooking the fields and woods.

The main house has a library and conservatory which visitors can use, and two different meditation rooms, including one with a huge golden Buddha by the window. The meditation space available for visitors night and day is the Dhamma Hall where mats, cushions, blankets and chairs cater for knees and joints of every condition. Starting or ending a visit here with an unguided meditation in the hall is highly recommended. In Dhamma Hall you'll find books for 'free distribution' with titles like *Clarity and Calm for Busy People*. The Buddhists here clearly know their audience.

Not charging for food, books and short residential stays may be one of the key practices of Theravada, but Chithurst Monastery relies on donations, so please remember to give back if you can.

Also worth knowing is that as part of the monastery's weekly timetable Mondays are silent days. Pujas (worship rituals) are held most evenings at 7.30pm (except Mondays and Fridays) when a monk or nun is at hand should you have any pressing questions or be facing any existential dilemmas.

See Walk 4, page 66.

SACRED BUILDINGS, HOMES & COMMUNITIES

English Martyr's Church sistinechapeluk.co.uk english-martyrs.co.uk
Goring Way, Goring-by-Sea, West Sussex BN12 4UH
Open: April to October Monday–Friday.

One of the county's best-kept secrets is this unassuming Catholic church on the edge of Goring-by-Sea. It may look like little more than a converted barn from the outside (it is) but inside the English Martyr's Church boasts the world's only full reproduction of the Sistine Chapel ceiling, over two-thirds the size of the original. What's more, it is a truly superb replica, capturing and matching the colours and rich tableaux of Michelangelo's masterpiece, painted in the early 1500s.

Such a grandiose idea began in 1985 when local parishioner and sign-writer Gary Bevans took a pilgrimage to Rome, met the Pope and visited the Sistine Chapel. Returning home, it occurred to him that the ceiling of his own local church was somewhat plain in comparison. And so a plan began to form. Unsurprisingly, when he put his proposal to the bishop there were initial hesitations. For one thing Gary had no formal training in art. But after making a series of small reproductions on 8x4 panels in his back garden he convinced the church to let him go ahead. Originally Gary had planned to do it the easy way – first paint onto boards and then fix them to the ceiling. This, however, proved to damage the work in the process so instead he attached the boards to the ceiling and, Michelangelo-style, painted onto the ceiling direct. For five and a half years – in between full-time work and family duties – Gary could be found up scaffolding, paint brush in hand and fantasising about neck massages. Over the years he would paint over 500 figures and 6 miles (10 kilometres) of straight lines. To help with costs he was sponsored by Dulux; spiritual guidance came in the form of holy water mixed with his paints. The official unveiling took place on 5th November 1993 after a mass of thanksgiving where Gary was presented with the papal cross *Pro Ecclesia et Pontifical*. Decades on, he is now deacon of the church but can still be found in there on occasion, doing touch-ups.

The English Martyr's Church is free to see. Visitors are even provided with a mirror-topped trolley to push around to view the ceiling (and to save you getting neck ache). On a sunny day, the church's beautiful modernist stained glass combined with Bevans' ceiling can make for a transcendent experience.

St Botolph's Church
Hardham nr Pulborough, West Sussex RH20 1LB

Just off the main road close to Pulbrough – and not far from the Coldwaltham Yew – this pretty Saxon church is home to the oldest and most complete series of frescos, dating back to roughly 1100 CE. Stepping inside is to enter a 1,000-year-old gallery of biblical-themed wall paintings in their distinctive 'egg and bacon' colour scheme. The frescos, discovered in the mid-19th century when plaster was chipped off the chancel arch, cover the entirety of the church walls on two tiers and would once have been accompanied by explanatory inscriptions in their borders – a bit like a cartoon but perhaps without the pithy punchlines. Subjects covered include the Nativity, the massacre of the innocents, the legend of St George and the torments of Hell. Best preserved are the figures of Adam and Eve which to some might be slightly reminiscent of Picasso's *Girls of Avignon* with their angular bodies, contorted necks and shapely bellies. Owing to this affected style being found in other artwork in Sussex from the same period suggests that it may all have been created by the same team of itinerant artists. That Adam and Eve are sporting huge belly buttons, however, suggests that said creators really should have paid more attention at Sunday School.

Coombes Church
Coombes Farm, Lancing, West Sussex BN15 0RS
Open: 9.30am–4pm

Remotely set on a 1,000-acre (405-hectare) farm, this small, humble rectangular building is, like St Botolph's, another Saxon church, believed to have been built around the 11th and 12th century.

Unusually this Grade I listed church stands on sloping hillside within Coombes Farm which itself is only 100 or so years old, suggesting that in medieval times the church originally served the long-since vanished hamlet of Coombes. Its isolation, however, doubtless helped preserve some of its interior artwork which, like St Botolph's, is medieval and was discovered in the 20th century. Again too, images depict the Nativity and other stories from the gospels used as pictorial teachings for parishioners who could not read. What is truly stunning in the church's barn-like interior is the detail of the artwork and vivid colours of reds, blues, yellows, ochre and pink. There is Christ giving the keys of heaven to St Peter and the book to St Paul, and a fearsome feathered creature which some suggest may be St John's eagle. If so, its creators were clearly unaware that birds only have two legs not four. Particularly unusual is a hunched figure – known as a caryatid – supporting one of the beams and, like St Botolph's Adam and Eve, bears an almost Picasso-like quality to its composition and features. That this artwork is to be found in a church devoid of ornamentation, Gothic pomposity and elaborate furnishings may, for some, make for a richer deeper sense of the sacred amongst the Sussex landscape.

St Andrew's Church
Bishopstone, East Sussex BN25 2UD

Here in the quiet little village of Bishopstone, just outside the coastal town of Seaford, lies the site of the long-forgotten, only female Sussex saint – St Lewinna – in the church of St Andrew's. Though faded from historical memory, her story holds a timeless resonance, offering a unique source of inspiration, especially for today's young women.

St Lewinna was an early Sussex Saxon Christian, having converted before St Wilfrid made his famous conversions in the last stronghold of the pagan South Saxon lands. She was martyred as a teenager in 670 CE, killed by violent means such as a blow to her head by a sword or axe. After burial, her grave became a magnet for pilgrims seeking healing from this holy virgin who stood firm in her faith. Three hundred years after her death, her bones were dug up, and a new shrine was built as an extension to the Saxon church minster, which can still be seen today, as the porch to the church. Inside is a recess where a statue would have once stood, most likely to the saint. Her fame for miracle healing and cures spread far and wide. In 1058, Balgar, a Flemish monk from the abbey of St Winoc in Bergues, Flanders (now France), was blown off course in a storm and landed at Seaford. He decided he would liberate St Lewinna's relics, and take her bones back to his abbey, where she would gain greater fame and help more people. Some of her bones were left behind in his haste to flee. Perhaps they were reburied in the graveyard where they remain to this day. Over in Flanders, her bones were venerated at the abbey until the French Revolution when it was sacked. Her thigh bone survived the ruins and was moved to the local town church, St Martin's. There they remained until the church was bombed in the Second World War. The theft of St Lewinna's bones adds an intriguing layer to her narrative. Despite this theft, the energy of the shrine persists, a testament to the resilience of a young woman who defied the norms of her time.

A visit to St Andrew's Church and the site of the shrine is a must. The church is a pretty treasure trove, containing a rare Sussex Sheela-na-gig on the Norman church tower, ancient medieval graffiti and the grave of another forgotten but once famous 1920s society clairvoyant, actress, author and probable WWII spy, Nell St John Montague. She predicted the death of Lord Kitchener a few weeks before he died at sea in 1916 and helped solve a gruesome Eastbourne 'Crumbles' murder in 1924 with her psychic powers. With its panoramic views, a fantastic circular walk up to Rookery Hill enhances the experience as you gaze down on the church and village, and out to the Seaford cliffs and dramatic coastline. The landscape provides a glimpse into the vistas St Lewinna might have admired as she walked these lands.

Her story transcends the centuries, embodying resilience, faith and defiance of societal norms. In an era where young women still navigate complex challenges, St Lewinna becomes an icon, encouraging them to stand firm in their beliefs and embrace their sense of self. As we tread the same paths she once walked, we rediscover a forgotten saint and draw inspiration from her indomitable spirit. St Lewinna's legacy, rekindled amidst the ancient Saxon stones, invites us to reflect on stories of enduring strength found within these hidden corners of Sussex herstory.

St Richard's Church

Burton Park, near Duncton, West Sussex GU28 0QU

Located in the grounds of Burton Park Estate, but accessible to the public, this small Norman church is home to an extraordinary 16th-century mural. By the north nave window, a robed female figure being crucified upside down on a diagonal cross can be seen. This shocking image is thought to be of St Wilgefortis, or St Uncumber, as she became known in England. Wilgefortis was a 14th-century Portuguese princess who vowed to become a nun rather than marry a man chosen by her father. She prayed to be made so unattractive that the man would never marry her, and her wish was granted when she grew a beard. Her enraged father had her crucified. This story became popular in the Netherlands, Germany and Austria in the 15th century, but she was never depicted crucified upside down. The X-shaped cross of the Sussex fresco may therefore represent a conflation with St Catherine, whose 'torture wheel' inspired the name for the Catherine's Wheel spinning firework. St Uncumber was prayed to by those seeking freedom from encumbrances. One source tells us 'the saint is said to have inspired particular devotion among men seeking release from their wives', another tells us that she was appealed to by women who wished to be liberated – unencumbered – from abusive husbands. Much of folk magic practice in old times – and even today – revolves around either attracting more of something (primarily health, love or wealth) or repelling something (disease, enemies or tedious partners). St Richard's Church is perhaps a good place to visit if you are seeking the latter kind of liberation.

Berwick Church

See Walk 6, page 73.

Steyning Church
See Walk 8, page 83.

Wilmington Church
See Walk 6, page 73.

Meeting House
Sussex University Campus, Falmer, nr Brighton BN1 9RH

This elegant circular building nestled amongst trees in the heart of Sussex University campus by Falmer is a Modernist triumph of glass, copper and concrete. An inter-denominational place of worship it was designed by Basil Spence – best known as the architect for Coventry Cathedral – and was amongst the last major structures to be built as part of the campus in the 1960s, after Spence realised that the university had made no provisions for a place of worship. The building's most dazzling features are a complex array of 460 panes of coloured glass and a decidedly psychedelic blue 'eye' ceiling light in the chapel which wouldn't look out of place in the opening credits of *The Twilight Zone*. It has been placed at an angle in the conical roof of the building so that the light shines through it directly onto the altar. Stepping into this building when the morning or evening sun is low and radiating rich colours across the chapel can make for an enchanting experience. (Though rest assured, even on the dullest day this is a building with the power to lift the spirits.)

While multifunctional and used by the university for everything from choir rehearsals to a social space, the Meeting House's Quiet Room is always available to those seeking solace from the world outside. For meditation, prayer or simply as a place of architectural awe it remains one of Sussex's most overlooked gems.

The Sanctuary
Washington, West Sussex RH20 3JD. Veras Walk & Sanctuary Lane

A 12-minute drive from Steyning brings you to Washington, a village just outside Storrington where Vera Pragnell (1897–1968) tried to create a spiritual and artistic community on 27 acres (11 hectares) of land she bought with her inheritance. Inspiration came in the form of a radical strand of Christianity and the philosophy of Edward Carpenter – an early champion of gay rights, sexual liberation, nudism and utopian socialism. Having travelled to the site on her donkey from her home in Surrey, Pragnell invited anyone who wished to create a more peaceful and spiritual life to live in the community, giving them half an acre on which to build a simple house or park a caravan. Pragnell established the Sanctuary as 'a queer place in which a queer conglomeration of people congregate'. In this she succeeded. Regulars included the British Communist Party, a phallus-worshipping health guru who named himself after Dionysius and one individual who claimed that Aleister Crowley had once turned him into a camel. (He 'got better'.) For a while the project flourished, with a school, a shop and a building used for theatre and dance performances. Forty to fifty people lived there at any one time, with a waiting list of hundreds who wanted to sample this utopian life. Visitors could buy crafts made by community members and a tea shop was established. The poet Victor Neuburg and Edward Carpenter supported the project but by 1932, after only a decade, Pragnell closed the whole thing down. Tabloids had run stories of 'bohemian' goings-on and made much of the nudity, which formed part of the utopian ideals of freedom of expression espoused by Carpenter and others. The pressure from this publicity, combined with most members being hopelessly impractical, and Pragnell's insistence on avoiding any guiding philosophy or credo, meant there was not enough to hold the community together and the dream died. Visiting the area now, known to locals as 'Sleepy Hollow', you might still feel the potential of this dream as you follow the small roads Veras Walk and Sanctuary Lane, wander past her home at Sanctuary Cottage and across the road to the small memorial garden and wooden shelter commemorating the community.

Blake's Cottage *blakecottage.org*
1 Blake's Road, Felpham, Bognor Regis, West Sussex PO22 7EB

One of Britain's greatest mystics was William Blake (1757–1827), a visionary artist and poet best known for *Songs of Innocence and Experience* and, as biographer John Higgs puts it, 'author of the unofficial English national anthem "Jerusalem" and a rare, inclusive symbol of English identity'. A seminal time in Blake's life was spent in Sussex. In 1800, exhausted and in penury in London, he accepted an offer from a more successful poet and friend, William Hayley, to live in a thatched cottage that Hayley owned in Felpham, West Sussex, on the outskirts of Bognor Regis. During the three years that Blake and his wife spent in Felpham, the artist wrote the poem 'Jerusalem' which Hubert Parry, living in the nearby village of Rustington, set to music as a hymn in 1916. He also produced eighteen portraits of poets for Hayley's library, numerous illustrations for Hayley's works, and began work on his epic poem *Milton*.

At first Blake adored Felpham, writing to a friend: 'Our cottage is beautiful. If I should ever build a palace it would only be my cottage enlarged... The sweet air and voices of winds, trees and birds, and the odours of the happy ground, makes it a dwelling for immortals.' He also 'witnessed' a fairy funeral while walking alone in their Felpham garden, writing: 'There was a great stillness among the branches and flowers and more than a common sweetness in the air. I heard a low and pleasant sound and I know not whence it came. At last I saw the broad leaf of a flower move and underneath I saw a procession of creatures, of the size and colour of green and grey grasshoppers, bearing a body laid out in a roseleaf, which they buried with sings and then disappeared. It was a fairy's funeral.' Sadly, over the three years that Blake lived in the seaside village, he grew frustrated with his lot. Hayley was working him too hard and the last straw arrived when Blake got into an altercation with a drunken soldier, ending with him having to defend himself in court against the soldier's accusation that he had uttered words that amounted to high treason. Blake was acquitted and he returned to live out the rest of his life in London.

While a plaque proclaims its famous resident, at the time of writing the cottage can only be viewed from the outside. For four centuries it was a private dwelling. Now it is owned by the Blake Cottage Trust with long-term plans for a full restoration for visitors to see the interior of the cottage – as it would have been – and even to sleep there.

A few minutes' walk from Blake's Cottage, pass the Fox Inn – where another plaque records the site of his scuffle with the soldier – and turn left into Limmer Lane to find St Mary's Church which displays two contemporary stained-glass windows created by Meg Lawrence in 2011. These are extraordinarily accomplished works of art depicting two angels of creation holding orbs. One celebrates human love, the sky and sea. The other depicts beasts of the forest, including the tiger inspired by Blake's poem 'The Tyger' – 'Tyger Tyger burning bright'. Below the angels are the immortal words of Blake's poem: 'To see a world in a grain of sand/ And a heaven in a wild flower/ Hold infinity in the palm of your hand/ And eternity in an hour.' At the base of the window are exquisite representations of the Felpham cottage with the sea behind, and a Van Gogh-like scene of a crescent moon above a sea of wheat with a windswept tree in the foreground.

SUSSEX VISIONARIES

A WITCH, A WIZARD & A SAINT

Sussex has long been a hotspot for religious communities, occult groups, utopianists, seekers and gurus. East Grinstead in the Ashdown Forest has even earned itself a reputation as Britain's strangest town, with a whole range of religious and spiritual organisations having headquarters or establishments in or near the town that are run by Scientologists, Rosicrucians, Mormons, members of Opus Dei and Rudolf Steiner's Anthroposophic Movement. Twenty minutes down the road from here Lewes, amongst many other things, is home to one of the UK's largest Subud groups, a spiritual movement based around the teachings of an Indonesian guru that utilises a unique form of spiritual practice known as latihan (from an Indonesian term *latihan kejiwaan* meaning 'spiritual exercise').

In 1944 one of the most controversial figures to have ever ended up in Sussex was Aleister 'The Great Beast' Crowley. A proponent of sex-magic and founder of the religion of Thelema, Crowley championed individualism and 'magick', and participated in complex occult rituals. He could also be something of a monster and would have been a royal pain in the arse to share a flat with. His autumn years were spent living in a boarding house in Hastings, addicted to heroin. Unwilling to allow Crowley's ashes to sully their town, the good folk of Hastings had him 'shipped over' to Brighton where, in December 1947, he was cremated in Woodvale Cemetery at a funeral that drew only twelve people.

Crowley would have been well known to Vera Pragnell; a very different kind of spiritual visionary of the early 20th century who spent ten years running her proto-hippy community close to Steyning (see pages 46–47).

Together with its cults and communes, Sussex has also inspired extraordinary visionary writing from the likes of Richard Jefferies, Hilaire Belloc and of course, William Blake. But as we're limited by space, it seems only fitting that this section pays tribute to two singular Sussex saints, and the only witch in Britain to have her own blue plaque.

The Saint of Sussex

Bosham may be a small, sleepy coastal village a few miles west of Chichester but it does lay claim to quite a few extraordinary names and events from history and myth. Legend has it that Canute the Great (c. 990–1035) had a palace in the village and it was here, hubristically, that he commanded those stubborn waves to clear off. Bosham is also believed to be both birth and burial place of the last Saxon king: Harold II (1022–66). It was here too that Harold received blessings before heading off to Hastings and the village gets name-checked in the Bayeux Tapestry in relation to a meeting between Harold and Edward the Confessor. Less well known these days is Bosham's former resident and spiritual teacher Henry Thomas Hamblin (1873–1958), once known as the 'Saint of Sussex'.

For the early part of his adult life in London, Hamblin was a successful optician by day, mystic by night, though as far as he was concerned the spiritual life and the practical life were inseparable. Suffering from both divine visions and night terrors, when Hamblin gave up his successful business the nightmares stopped, confirming his belief that the spiritual path was sacred and true. Hamblin retired to Bosham, wrote a series of lessons on spiritual development, and then when he received further illumination, dug a hole in the garden and burnt them all. He then wrote a new improved version, *The Way of the Practical Mystic*, as a complete spiritual course in 26 lessons. Hamblin mixed Christianity with ideas from the nascent New Age and psychotherapy, his key principle being that we can change our lives for the better by positive thinking and changing habits based around selfishness and instant gratification. He was also ahead of his time in teaching a form of mindfulness. Such was Hamblin's reputation on the 'spiritual circuit' that when Indian philosopher and saint Swami Ramdas (1884–1963) and his disciple Mother Krishnabai (1903–89) went on a world tour in 1954 they made a point of meeting him. Hamblin's ideas and teachings continue through the Hamblin Trust, though its beautiful retreat centre, once based in Bosham, no longer exists.

Doreen Valiente: High Priestess of Modern Witchcraft

Where else but Brighton would lay claim to the UK's only blue plaque to honour a bona fide witch? On the side of a council estate building close to an area known as Kemp Town (Tyson Place, Grosvenor Street BN2 0JQ) the plaque proclaims: 'Doreen Valiente (1922–99), poet, author and mother of modern witchcraft, lived here'.

For Valiente it all began with a mystical encounter at the age of nine when, living in London, she felt the presence of something hidden and mysterious in her garden. It sent her on a lifelong journey into the occult, first scouring her local library and second-hand bookshops for tomes on witchcraft in her early teens. After working as a translator at Bletchley Park during the war she would eventually come to hear of a modern-day coven in Hertfordshire established by the occultist Gerald Gardner. She joined the coven and soon became its High Priestess. While it was Gardner who gave his name to much of our modern-day take on witchcraft – and the global movement that would eventually become known as Wicca – it was Valiente who helped produce some of the key texts including 'The Witches' Rune' and 'Charge of the Goddess', bringing a sense of litany to coven practice. 'Charge of the Goddess' is considered by many to be Valiente's most important written contribution to Wicca and paganism: in poetic form it invokes the feminine deity and is still used worldwide in Wiccan ceremonies. Over the decades, Valiente would increasingly voice her beliefs in feminism, sex education and environmentalism, not just within the Wiccan movement but to the wider world. Throughout the 1960s she practised with different covens, made several appearances on television and wrote a book, *Where Witchcraft Lives* (1962), exploring the history of witchcraft in Sussex. In 1970 she moved to Brighton and helped found The Pagan Front, a pressure group dedicated to campaigning for Wicca and other pagan practices to be accepted as genuine religions. Flirtations with far-right groups in this period somewhat temper Valiente's legacy, though it is not without grounds that some suggest that she had infiltrated as a government spy and quit one group citing their homophobia and sexism as her reasons for her leaving.

She remains the most influential and inspiring woman in neo-paganism and Wicca which, in some ways, can be considered a close cousin of druidry, honouring the Eightfold Wheel of the Year and the cycles of life and using ritual magic for personal and planetary transformation. The Sussex landscape played a key role in Valiente's life and in her rituals. In many photos she sports beads, huge owl glasses and terrific hats, looking every bit the bohemian and mysterious auntie who, when you were little, seemed slightly terrifying but that you secretly looked forward to visiting.

PART TWO

NINE WALKS EXPLORING THE MAGIC LANDSCAPE OF SUSSEX

We've chosen nine walks that allow you to experience some of the magic of the Sussex landscape with sacred and historical spots as focal points along the way. Nine feels a good number – sacred to the Goddess, and signifying idealism, selfless giving and humanitarianism. You could treat these nine walks as pilgrimages: you could undertake them with intention so that they raise your spirits and feed your soul, or if that sounds too earnest, you can follow these walks simply as a way of getting to know Sussex in all its variety: from her chalk cliffs to the High Weald, from her Levels to the great plain that stretches between the North and South Downs known in Saxon times as the 'Waste of Ondred'.

Taking a walk on a significant date in the year can make a walk feel special – more memorable somehow. Our family invite all our friends to walk with us every New Year's Day, and this has become a tradition now going back over twenty years. We finish the walk with a party, which marks the end of the festive season that began just before Christmas at the winter solstice. If, twenty years ago, we had resolved to invite all our friends on a walk at least once a year, but with no set date chosen, it probably wouldn't have happened in many years, since the days tend to run away with themselves, and it wouldn't have become a tradition.

So here's a suggestion: link your magical walks with a special day: a birthday, anniversary or one of the eight seasonal festivals which underpin both indigenous pre-Christian traditions in these lands and the Christian faith which has adopted these same festival times.

WALK 1

HILLFORTS & HIDDEN GEMS

CISSBURY RING & HIGHDOWN GARDENS

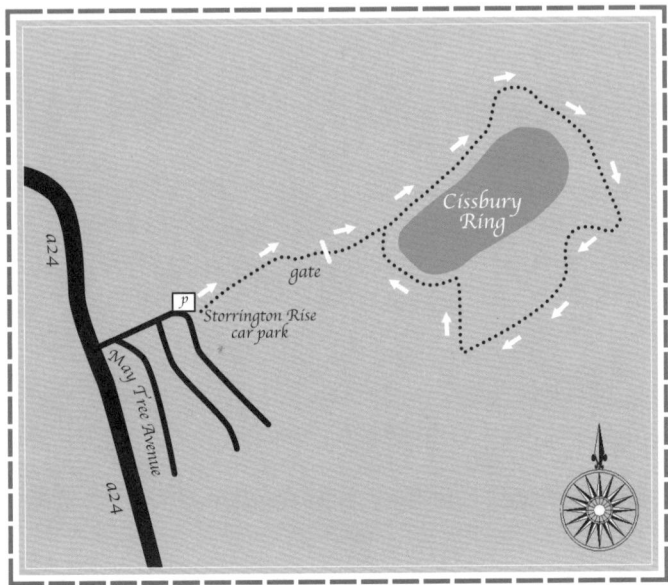

Summary
- **Start point:** Storrington Rise car park, Worthing BN14 0HU
- **Distance:** Circular around Cissbury Ring 2 miles (3.2 km)
- **Duration:** 1.5 hours
- **Description:** Hilly, open trail that can be muddy after rainfall
- **Refreshments:** Highdown Gardens BN12 6FB
- **Transport:** Bus/car

Spend a half day exploring a part of West Sussex that offers astounding views from the largest hillfort in Sussex, and a hidden gem of a garden tucked into the chalk hillside nearby.

This part of Sussex isn't the most attractive. Swathes of bungalows can be seen on the lower slopes of insignificant-looking hills, and driving to Cissbury along the busy A24 is hardly romantic. But discovering magic is all about looking beyond surface appearances, and – like the alchemist – finding the gold in the dross.

❶ *Turn off the A24 at May Tree Avenue and head for Storrington Rise car park. From there walk directly up the hill ignoring other tracks that lead off to the right in different directions. On reaching the periphery of a small wooded area continue upwards, passing through a gate. Eventually you'll see the option to take the lower path around the hillfort, but for the best views head up through the gate and up the steps to the track that leads around the top ramparts. Magicians cast their circles clockwise, and in magical rites 'circumambulate' (walk in a circle) clockwise too. So you might like to do this on your walk, turning left to walk around the site. Soon you'll see a fenced-off area that protects you, and the wild ponies that roam here, from falling into the remnants of a Neolithic flint mine.*

As you walk around the fort, imagine the centuries of life that animated this huge area that covers about 60 acres (24 hectares). The fort was built in the Iron Age, around 250 BCE, and abandoned around 50 CE, so for three centuries families lived and died here, their spirits still lingering perhaps, admiring the views out towards the sea, from Brighton in the east to the Isle of Wight in the west. And in the great sweep of land from west to east via the north, they – and you now – can see the great flatland of the Waste of Ondred that stretches from the River Rother in Kent to the Meon Valley in Hampshire. They – and now you – can see those hilltops that acted as beacons for travellers and housed settlements or ancient barrows, including Lancing Ring and Highdown Hill. With such a magnificent panorama, no wonder our ancestors chose to live and defend themselves from this vantage point.

❷ *Continue around the circumference until you reach your starting point.*

It takes about an hour to walk around the fort but the interior might now beckon you to enter, perhaps to picnic beneath a tree or – on quieter days – to meditate or simply be still. Give yourself an hour and a half for this walk to take account of this possibility, which will be even more attractive if you are walking on a summer's day.

❸ *Return the way you came.*

Optional extra

If you arrived by car you have the option to continue your exploration by driving for 20 minutes to Highdown Gardens. Again, like the alchemist, you'll be plunged back into the leaden world of the mundane – of roads and dreary urbanisation – only to discover another nugget of gold in the Downs. Here – in just 8 acres/ 3 hectares – you'll encounter in a more obvious way a fact that applies to the whole of the South Downs National Park – that this is an area that is more diverse, in terms of plant species, than the Amazon rainforest.

❹ *Park in the car park that you reach by driving up Highdown Rise, having turned off the A259. Go past the Highdown hotel car park on the left and continue up to the public car park a few metres further up the hill. The entrance to Highdown Gardens is beside the car park, and all at once you will find yourself in a magical world of rare flowers and trees.*

The gardens were the creation of two unusual aristocrats, Sir Frederick and Lady Sybil Stern, who from 1909 to 1967 dedicated most of their energies into creating a paradise out of an old chalk pit and a few acres of land that surrounded their house, which is now the Highdown hotel – a good spot for lunch after your walk.

Over more than half a century the Sterns developed what has now been nominated a National Plant Collection: a unique and rare collection of plants gathered from around the world that includes many species not commonly found in the UK – and all with the aim of discovering which plants would thrive on chalk soil. With a sensory garden, a visitor's centre offering information on the collection and a host of tranquil dells, Highdown provides the perfect place to meditate on the ways in which we can co-operate and interact with nature to bring more beauty into the world, and of how having a love and a focus – an obsession even, if carefully tended – can lead to a lasting legacy for future generations.

WALK 2

ANCIENT YEWS & HILLTOP BARROWS

FROM KINGLEY VALE
TO THE DEVIL'S HUMPS

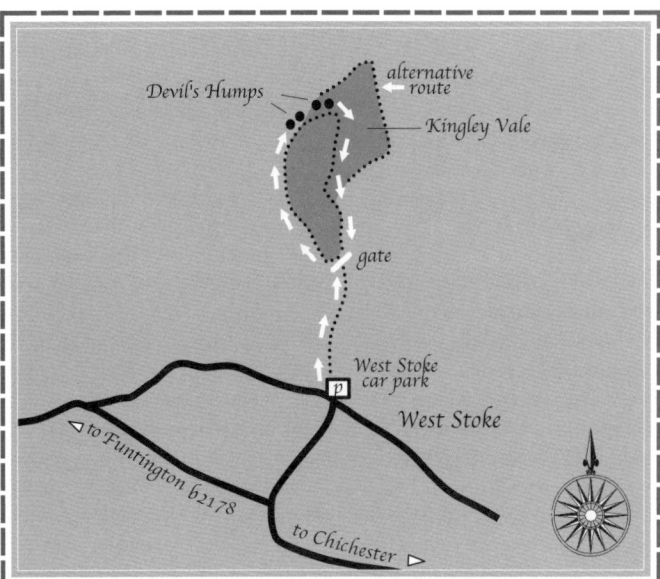

Summary
- **Start point:** West Stoke car park, 10 minutes drive from Chichester PO18 9BE
- **Distance:** Circular 3–4 miles (4.8–6.4 km)
- **Duration:** 1.5–2 hours
- **Description:** Hilly forest trail with some steep steps and muddy paths after rainfall
- **Refreshments:** The Anchor Bleu in Bosham PO18 8LS
- **Transport:** Car only

Deep in West Sussex, Kingley Vale is home to the largest yew forest in Europe within which a grove of ancient yews are amongst the oldest living beings in Britain. This circular trail takes you into one of the most enchanted forests you will encounter; with stunning views of the countryside and coastline, and is home to one of the most important concentrations of well-preserved archaeological sites in southern England.

[59]

WALK 2

❶ *Start from the West Stoke car park. From here walk for 15 minutes or so along the track that leads to the Kingley Vale Nature Reserve. Once you get to the reserve, go through the gate and take the track that is immediately to your left, running near the fence. By going this way around the circular route, you are conforming to the well-established practice in magic of walking clockwise around a sacred site. Before you do this, however, pay a visit to the Field Museum, just beyond the big wooden sculpture that announces the reserve.*

The Field Museum is an octagonal wooden hut with illustrations and text that share some of the fascinating history and geography of Kingley Vale. On the ceiling, paintings of owls and raptors illustrate the rich bird life found in this area which also include varieties of woodpeckers, finches, warblers and tits. All in all, over fifty species of birds can be found in this area, with thirty-nine species of butterfly alone recorded in the grassland of the reserve.

❷ *As you follow the path that leads you gradually uphill, you are skirting the younger yew trees of the forest. If you need a break halfway up, keep your eyes peeled for a reserve sign and dew pond on the left; there's a seat here with splendid views. Over the next half-hour you climb a couple of hundred metres in elevation but it's worth it: by the time you get to the crest of the ridge that curves around the northern boundary of the vale, you are treated to amazing views out to the coast. Make your way to the Devil's Humps, sometimes called the Kings' Graves. These are four barrows here that you can't miss and that look out over the yew forest below.*

The Devil's Humps are likely to date from the Late Neolithic or Early Bronze Age, although they may have been re-used in the Roman and Anglo-Saxon periods. These barrows represent some of the best examples of these types of structure across the South Downs. Some archaeologists believe that they may have once been covered with chalk and would have appeared as glowing white beacons, visible for miles. In legend, they house the bones of druids or of Viking warriors, perhaps of Danes who raided this part of Sussex in the 9th century. Climbing to the top feels essential — certainly the top of each of the two bigger mounds, known as 'bell barrows'. Your view from the summits on a clear day will be spectacular: open vistas of rolling countryside to the north, and then to the south the beautiful green sward and thick forest of Kingley Vale directly below you, with Chichester Harbour, Hayling Island and the open sea stretching into the distance. On a particularly clear day you may be able to spot the spire of Chichester Cathedral far away and over to the left and, over to your right, the Isle of Wight.

Should you wish to conduct a simple ceremony in this sacred place, take one of the many chalk stones lying around here and – as you will see others have done – place it in one of the hollows in the ground. You could do this with the intention of honouring the memory of an ancestor or lost loved one, just as you might do when lighting a candle in a church.

❸ *From the top of the humps look for a path ahead of you that deviates to the left of the main path. This will take you on a wide sweep around the vale and add another 30 minutes to your walk. If you don't have the time, return to the main path and, with the humps on your left, look for a grassy path that deviates to the right. After about 100 yards (90 metres) along you will reach a fence and a kissing gate walk. The path will begin to sweep down towards the old forest that lies beyond the central green sward of the valley. Keep a look out on the right for a flight of steps to take you down to the vale. The descent is demanding and sometimes slippery but soon you'll be approaching one of the most magical and enchanting forests you will encounter anywhere on the planet.*

In ancient times the yew was steeped in folklore and magic and believed to have the power to ward off evil spirits and to symbolise eternal life. The yew was also considered a powerful symbol of death and resurrection owing to the ability for the drooping branches of old trees that reach the ground to take root and form new trunks. Nowadays it is most strongly associated with church graveyards having been incorporated into Christian mythology, where it was said that their presence would protect the dead – certainly from cattle and other animals that avoid grazing near yews. It's always worth remembering that many parts of the tree are highly poisonous – especially the needles and the berry's seeds; one of the authors of this book made himself unwell the first time he visited Kingley Vale after overzealously fondling the needles of a branch. A small child who eats yew needles can become severely ill. Some of the yews here are believed to be at least over 500 years old, though the absence of growth rings due to rotting make it hard to pinpoint the exact ages. They are likely to be mere youngsters compared to the UK's oldest yew found in Glen Lyon in Scotland, which is probably between 2,000 and 3,000 years old, though some believe it is even older.

❹ *As you approach the forest, avoid taking the obvious route that takes you round to the right. Instead, ask the spirit of this special place if you can be shown the way directly into the forest, and if your wish is granted you will soon find yourself facing one of the oldest trees in the wood, whose curving and twisting limbs will introduce you to this otherworldly region which you can navigate by following your intuition, and the occasional signs of a* *path that will lead you straight into the heart of this ancient grove of trees.*

Each yew you encounter looks so unique, so strangely beautiful. Every so often they will cluster to form natural areas for ceremony, meditation or worship, or just a picnic.

❺ *Keep wandering through the woodland. If you continue straight on you will reach the entrance to the reserve.*

It's worth noting that no mobile signal is available here whatsoever. Deviate from the trail and you will be lost forever in the Otherworld.

❻ *Once you reach the entrance, follow the same 15-minute track back to the car park.*

If you have time, make the 10-minute drive to Bosham. There you can visit the Saxon church where King Canute's daughter is buried, walk around the Quay and sit in the Anchor Bleu pub for a meal or a drink, as you look out over the tidal bay. Gazing out across the water at high tide as the sun sets and the birds come flying home offers one of the most serene and peaceful views you will find in Sussex.

WALK 3

A MEDITATION ON MORTALITY AT THE MARGINS OF BRIGHTON

THE CHATTRI & CLAYTON TUNNEL

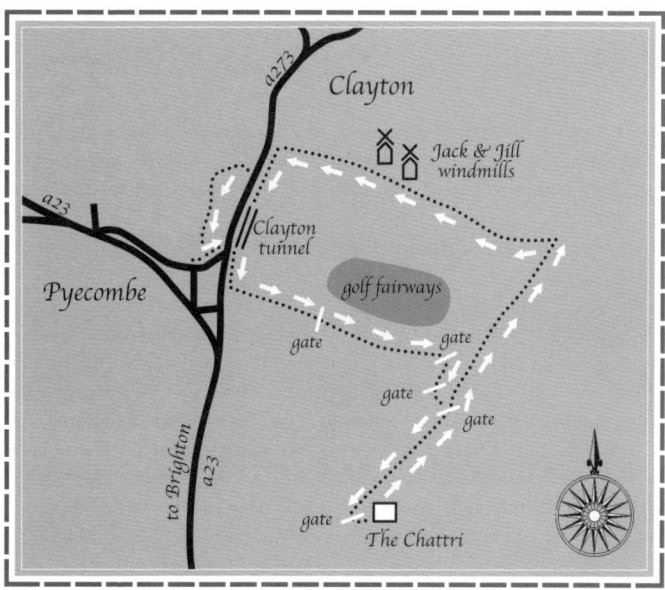

Summary
- **Start point:** Pyecombe village BN45 7FD, park on road by the crossroads next to the church
- **Distance:** Circular 5½ miles (9 km)
- **Duration:** 2.5–3 hours
- **Description:** Undulating, parts can be muddy after rain
- **Refreshments:** The Plough, BN45 7FN
- **Transport:** Bus/car

A few miles outside of Brighton, the ancient village of Pyecombe makes for the perfect starting point for a meditative stroll through Sussex downland. This gentle, unassuming landscape hides a unique, sacred memorial on the edge of the Downs: the Chattri. The walk ends with a folly that, while not quite sacred, inspired a very famous ghost story.

[63]

❶ *From Pyecombe church follow the South Downs Way east, descending School Lane at the crossroads down to the A273. Look for a gap in the hedge on the other side a few metres to the right and – being extra careful with fast-moving traffic here – cross the road. Follow a bridleway through a gate parallel with the road to the right. After 110 yards (100 metres) veer left through a gate ascending open land.*

In his passionate and mystical autobiography, *The Story of My Heart* (1883), written while living in Brighton, the Wiltshire-born author Richard Jefferies extols the benefits to the heart and soul of walking over the Downs: 'My heart was dusty, parched for want of the rain of deep feeling; my mind arid and dry... When this began to form I felt eager to escape from it...There is a hill to which I used to resort at such periods. The labour of walking three miles to it, all the while gradually ascending, seemed to clear my blood of the heaviness accumulated at home... I began to breathe a new air and to have a fresher aspiration.... Lying down on the grass I spoke in my soul to the earth, the sun, the air and the distant sea, far beyond sight.' Jefferies writes with the beating heart of a pagan.

❷ *Rejuvenated by the climb, continue into a wooded area via a gate, cross golf fairways and two fields to a tree line and wire fence. Turn right through a gate with a hedge on your right. After 110 yards (100 metres) the track turns left through a gate up the right side of a field. Enter the next gate on the right by way-marked arrows and descend a broad chalky track with Brighton and the English Channel far ahead of you. Soon a remarkable building will come into view in this empty landscape – the smooth dome of the Chattri. Make your way to it via another gate.*

Eerie, isolated and unique, the Chattri was built a century ago for Sikh and Hindu soldiers who died while hospitalised in Brighton during the First World War. Inscribed on the memorial in Hindi, Punjabi and English is written: 'In honour of these soldiers of the Indian Army whose mortal remains were committed to fire.' Here they were cremated, according to their religious rites, and their ashes scattered at sea. Granite slabs on the eastern side of the building mark the site of the three original pyres. An annual service is still held here every third Sunday in June. Those in attendance include the Brighton and Hove Hindu Elders Group, the mayor and local people. (For more details: chattri.org.)

Ironically, one of the reasons these soldiers were housed in Brighton Pavilion was based on the assumption they'd feel more at home with its 'Indian' style exterior. What they made of its kitsch over-the-top Oriental interior is anyone's guess!

❸ *Return to the wide chalky path and head north for 1½ miles (2.4 kilometres). At a T-junction turn left on a path that becomes Mill Lane, passing the iconic black and white Jack and Jill windmills on your right. Reaching the main road turn left along the pavement for 330 yards (300 metres) to a railway bridge. Peering over the wall will reveal the startling portal of the Clayton Tunnel – a 19th-century Gothic folly-cum-castle.*

Why this almost Disneyesque feature, complete with turrets and arrow slits, was built over the tunnel remains a mystery. And why the rail authorities later decided to build a cottage on top is an even greater mystery!

It was, however, the scene of a disastrous accident between two trains in 1861. Signal failure and a series of unfortunate misunderstandings led to the trains colliding inside the tunnel. It was noted too that the attendant signalman Killick had been compelled to work a 24-hour shift in order to earn himself a day off that week. In the hearing that followed he was not held responsible, but understandably his nerves never recovered. It was this accident that inspired Charles Dickens to write his second most famous 'Christmas' ghost story, *The Signalman* (1866).

❹ *Ruminating on the fragility and preciousness of life, retrace your steps up the road and turn left down a lane. About 220 yards (200 metres) on, veer left down a bridleway before rising through the woods in a long gradual climb. At the top traverse the crossroads and continue until the path becomes a drive, leading you back to Pyecombe and a well-earned rest at The Plough.*

In summer the open chalk downland here rings with the sound of skylarks, corn bunting, yellowhammers, goldfinch and the occasional squawk of a raptor. In winter you are more likely to hear the throaty screeches of corvids.

WALK 4

A MEDITATIVE MEANDER THROUGH MONASTIC WOODS

CHITHURST MONASTERY & LAKESIDE

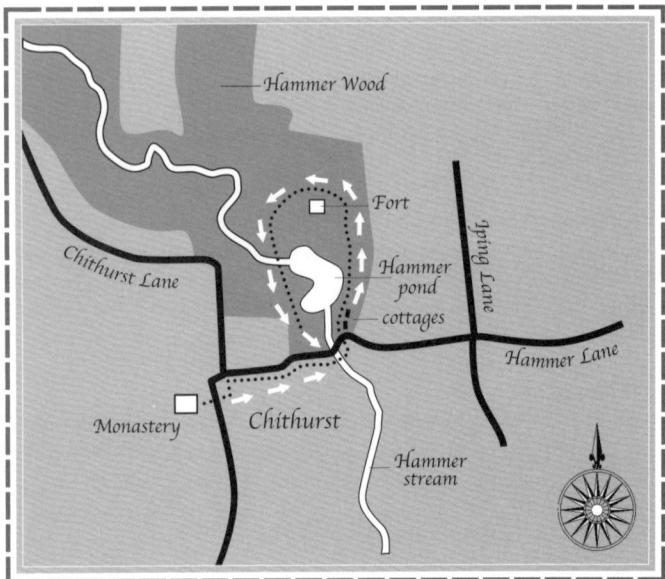

Summary
- **Start point:** Cittaviveka a.k.a Chithurst Buddhist Monastery car park, Petersfield GU31 5EU
- **Distance:** Circular 4 miles (6.4 km)
- **Duration:** 1.5 hrs (or allowing time for eating, meditating and visiting the monastery grounds, say 3 hours)
- **Description:** Moderately hilly parts, some paths can be muddy after rain
- **Refreshments:** Chithurst Monastery midday meal 10.30am (British Summer Time)/11.30am (winter) – check the website beforehand – and please remember to donate
- **Transport:** Car

Starting at the tranquil Chithurst Buddhist Monastery in the heart of a very leafy part of Sussex, this walk meanders through a woodland with a small waterfall and lake, past an ancient hillfort and along quiet country lanes before finishing back at Dhamma Hall and the opportunity for an unguided meditation in beautiful

Note
The monastery is only open to the public from April to December.

[66]

surroundings. Indeed, for those in need of some peace and stillness this entire walk may be undertaken as a silent meditation walk which, if timed well, could also include lunch at the monastery, evening pujas and a short consultation with a monk or nun.

For more details see Chithurst Monastery, pages 39–40.

❶ *From the main buildings and car park walk back down the path that you drove in on and turn left down a country lane. As it bends ignore the left turn and continue on, descending. After about ½ mile (0.8 kilometres) you'll pass two nuns' cottages: Rocana and Aloka. Cross a pretty stream over an old stone bridge and turn left into Hammer Wood.*

Hammer Wood – which took its name from a 17th-century forge – was first gifted to Cittaviveka in 1978 and was the catalyst for the order establishing a monastery here after the purchase of nearby Chithurst House the following year. This natural woodland is home to oak, silver birch, yew, ash, chestnut and hazel as well as different pine trees planted in the mid-20th century. Bird life is rich here too: nightjars, blackcaps, willow warblers, goldcrests, hobbies, kites, barn and tawny owls can all be seen and heard.

❷ *Continue on the path and after less than 55 yards (50 metres) you'll encounter something highly unusual for Sussex – a waterfall – followed shortly by gorgeous vistas across Hammer Pond.*

True, the waterfall is little more than 10 feet (3 metres) in height and manmade but it is still a rare and lovely thing to see in this part of England. The watering hole below looks to be an excellent place for wild swimming.

❸ *As you keep ascending and the path curves, to your right you come to the remains of a large Celtic hillfort, its presence only really sensed in the steep sides of the embankment.*

On the path you should by now have noticed a few 'Quiet Area' signs. These are to alert and remind us that we're on land owned by the monastery. Bear in mind that someone may well be staying in a residential hut nearby and, if you're not doing a silent walk, they might not appreciate you practising your tuba or having a member of your party who happens to have a laugh like a strangled donkey.

❹ *Continue along the path. At the end of May the paths here also take on a soft gossamer carpet of dandelion seed-heads. The stream should now re-appear on your left as you start to descend.*

Keep your eyes peeled too for Buddhist figurines and other symbolic statues and totems half hidden in tree trunks and walls.

5 *On seeing a wooden gate ignore the path just before it on the left. Go through the gate and descend immediately left down a path which can be muddy at times. At the bottom of the hill continue past Mike's Pond and cross Hammer Stream. The path now ascends and reaches a country lane. Turn left, then after just a few metres turn left again onto a public path. Follow the yellow footpath signs and descend into the woods again. As you reach the end of Hammer Wood look for the two nuns' cottages on your left and enter the lane, turn right and retrace your steps back to the monastery.*

Complete your woodland walk with a meditation in Dhamma Hall. If you're not used to meditation and find yourself wondering what to do with your mind as you sit in this peaceful place, you could try just feeling gratitude for the natural world and all its beauty, or the generosity of the monks and nuns at the monastery. Noticing the area in your body where you are feeling gratitude can then lead you to just following your breath, tracking it in your awareness as it flows in and out. And hey presto — you've been meditating!

WALK 5

FROM HIGH ROCKS TO HEALING WATERS

HIGH WEALD & TUNBRIDGE WELLS

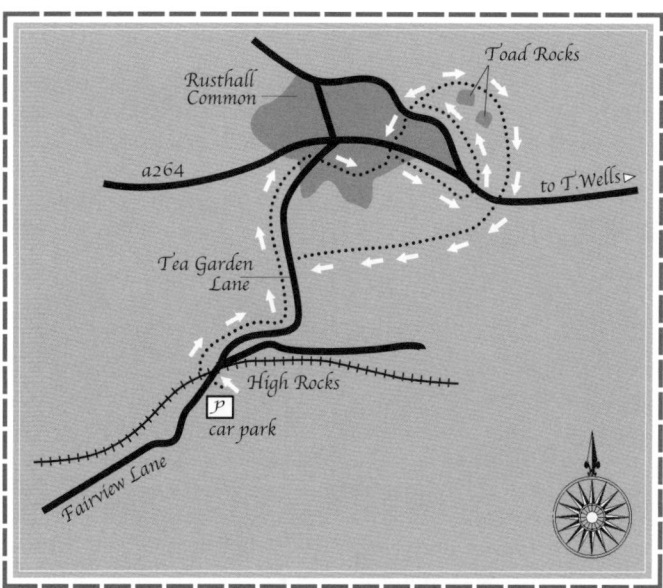

Summary
- **Start point:** High Rocks car park, Fairview Lane nr Tunbridge Wells TN3 9JJ
- **Distance:** Circular 5 miles (8 km)
- **Duration:** 2–3 hours, or longer if you visit Tunbridge Wells
- **Description:** Quiet lanes, commons, some steep steps, scrambling over rocks and muddy paths after rainfall
- **Refreshments:** High Rocks restaurant bar and/or the Pantiles, Tunbridge Wells
- **Transport:** Car or catch the Spa Valley Railway steam train from Tunbridge Wells, runs at weekends and Bank Holidays: spavalleyrailway.co.uk

Explore a remarkable and eerie world of sandstone rocks with spectacular views across the High Weald, and take a risk by venturing over the county border into darkest Kent. Here we encounter High Rocks, a toad stone and a healing spring; we picnic on the Devil's forehead and finish by exploring the elegance of Royal Tunbridge Wells.

WALK 5

Note

The High Rocks Monument – at the start of our walk – is privately owned and only open to the public from 10.15am until an unspecified time Wednesday–Sunday. It's always worth checking their website beforehand; they also close for private events, especially weddings in spring and summer. Even if High Rocks Monument is closed, there are plenty of other spectacular features in this walk to more than make up for it. Check about access before you go here: highrocks.co.uk.

❶ *Exit the car park and descend to the ivy-covered restaurant and bar to purchase a ticket that will allow you access to High Rocks. The entrance is across the road.*

The High Rocks Monument transports you to the world of our Stone Age ancestors, some of whom lived in the gulleys and atop the rocks. Spend a while in the seven or so acres, following the trail through the chasms and over the crags exploring this extraordinary scenery, with its magnificent views. On a balmy hot day here, this landscape might also evoke a similar supernatural otherworldliness to Peter Weir's 1975 folk horror classic *Picnic at Hanging Rock*. Here we are in a thin place, a porous landscape imbued with mystery (visitors notwithstanding). If any willowy Victorian teenager daughters are accompanying you on this walk it's best not to let them wander off.

❷ *When you've drunk in enough of these sacred rocks, exit, take a right and walk down Fairview Lane, go over the bridge – eyes and ears alert for a steam train – and take the first left continuing up Tea Garden Lane for about ½ mile (0.8 kilometres). You have now crossed over into Kent.*

Halfway up Tea Garden Lane on the right look for the Beacon, a wedding venue with an unusual history as a place of sanctuary for Basque and Jewish refugees. It's worth pausing here to look out over the countryside from this vantage point.

❸ *Continue up the lane and, before reaching the A264, turn right onto the commons, taking the upper path.*

Should you have brought a picnic for this walk – and why wouldn't you? – or just fancy a rest, look for a (hanging) rock outcrop on the right not too far along the path and close to a park bench. When the sun is shining this offers fabulous views over Happy Valley and the Weald. You'll be sitting in the same spot that our Neolithic ancestors would have done 10,000 years ago, doubtless admiring the view and munching on a gooseberry and turnip-flavoured snack bar.

❹ *Keep following the main upper path, passing more rocks on your right. The path eventually reaches a T-junction with wooden fencing and vehicle-blocking metal bars on the right. Take the left path,* following the fence to St Paul's Church graveyard and bear right following the green footpath sign, passing houses to reach the A264/Langton Road. Carefully cross the road after Rusthall Place. Head down Rusthall Road and Harmony Street to reach our next sacred outcrop: Toad Rock.

Here you find yourself in another uniquely strange spot. The huge toad-shaped rock is just one of many in this area of sandstone formations and is another perfect spot for a picnic. On the theme of toads, let's hope that those in Kent were spared the attentions of the toadmen and toadwitches, who lived further north in the Fens and Lincolnshire up until the 19th century. These 'cunning men and women' or folk wizards would catch toads, kill them and use their bones in their magic to effect cures or control humans or animals. Toad Rock itself baffled early geologists for many decades. Some even believed it to be the weathered remains of an ancient manmade sphinx, a fanciful notion that inspired H.G. Wells to reference it in his 1925 novel, *Christina Alberta's Father*.

While here, it's well worth exploring Upper Street – in front of the Toad Rock Retreat pub – all the way to the end at Eagles Terrace where another similar-looking rock towers right beside the front door of someone's house as if it's been slowly creeping up on them in a centuries-old game of What's the time, Mr Wolf?

❺ *Return to the front of Toad Rock by the sand, cross Harmony Street and follow a footpath up and over until it feels like you're heading down someone's drive then veer right through the woods on a path into a disused quarry.*

Named after a 19th-century quarryman, Bull's Hollow has remained disused since 1890 but is a popular spot today for climbers and is another place where these ancient rocks can have an almost supernatural presence.

❻ *At the end of Bull's Hollow take a path back to Rusthall Road and cross the A264. Look for the green footpath sign by Rusthall Place and retrace your steps back to St Paul's Church. Keeping it on your left, return to the T-junction and metal bars and now take the lower path through the common, descending with the rocks on your right and passing over Cold Bath Steps. Soon you'll ascend a sandy path that becomes wooden steps.*

While on this path look for the Devil's horns on your right – two great old trees growing either side of a stone outcrop on the upper path. If you stopped for food or a rest as recommended on your first venture across the commons, you would have been sitting right above this path on Beelzebub's forehead. Any devilish thoughts that came to mind while chomping on a cucumber sandwich back then can now be explained away.

❼ *Return down Tea Garden Lane, cross the bridge and either return to the car park or — if you're feeling adventurous — veer left onto the circular lower path around the High Rocks. With the railway line on your left after about 100 yards (90 metres) keep your eyes peeled for a place in the woods to scramble up to the top where you'll find yourself in a farmer's field. Turn right and follow the edge of the field with the woods on your right. Soon you'll reach the fenced perimeter of High Rocks. Keep on around the edge of the field until the fence ends and you find a path descending to the right. Head down into the wooded area, turn right on a main path and within 2 minutes you'll be at the car park.*

But wait! Have all your party returned? Or might some of them still be up on the rocks, wandering around like lost spirits in their starched cotton dresses and corsets…?

Extended walk
For an extended walk to Tunbridge Wells and its famed waters follow steps 8 and 9.

❽ *Should you have enough energy in you, turn left down High Rocks Lane until you get to Cabbage Stalk Lane on your right. Take that and soon this quiet lane will become a footpath that leads you through Tunbridge Wells Common until you get to cross the road and enter the Pantiles — a charming pedestrianised part of the town with plenty of restaurants and cafes.*

If you visit in the summer, you might be able to sample the chalybeate spring water served to you by a costumed 'dipper'. But even if you can't taste the water on the day you visit, you can see the well-head and the way the iron-rich water has stained the stones, just as you can at that other more famous source of chalybeate water, Chalice Well in Glastonbury.

❾ *When ready to leave the town, you have a 30-minute walk ahead of you. Retrace your steps, turning left out of Cabbage Stalk Lane into High Rocks Lane. After a while, you will have the opportunity to walk under the railway line that has been running to your left. You can either ignore this option and keep going along the lane, or you can take this path and follow the railway track on the other side, through the woods which eventually lead you to the ridge of sandstone that becomes High Rocks, with the car park ahead of you.*

WALK 6

WEAVING THE ANCESTORS' VOICES

THE LONG MAN OF WILMINGTON & BERWICK CHURCH

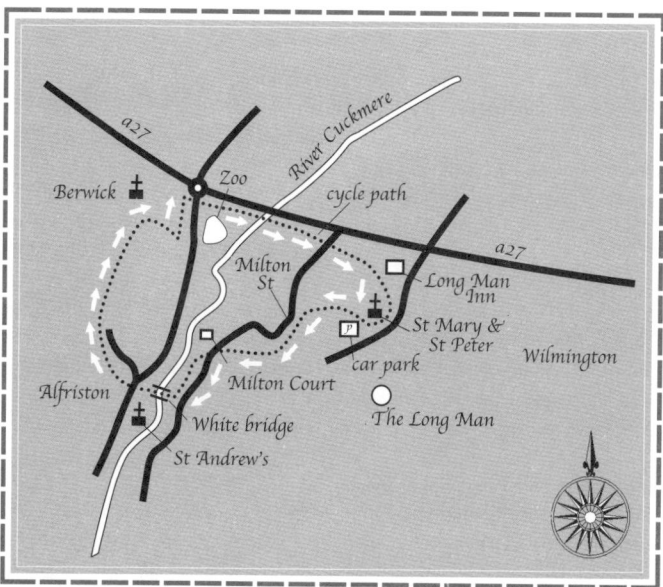

Summary

- **Start point:** Long Man car park, Wilmington village opposite the Long Man near BN26 5SL
- **Distance:** Circular 4–5 miles (6.4–8 km)
- **Duration:** 2–4 hours
- **Description:** Flat, open countryside and villages with some muddy paths after rainfall
- **Refreshments:** Long Man Inn, Wilmington, various pubs and eateries in Alfriston
- **Transport:** Car or take the train to Berwick to do the walk in a slightly different sequence

This walk across gently undulating Downland includes one of East Sussex's most beautiful villages, a stunning church whose interior was painted by members of the Bloomsbury Set, and starts at the enigmatic Long Man of Wilmington, ending at the inn named after him. Crucially it also follows sections of the Cuckmere Pilgrim Path, which could be walked with a clear intention in mind. Starting in the

[73]

small park beside the Long Man car park, with its magnificent view of the monument, you might like to begin your pilgrimage by asking this great chalk giant in the landscape for his or her (who can tell?) blessing. Standing with a stave in each hand, the Long Person you see before you suggests ideas of stability and balance – helpful qualities for any of us.

❶ *Leave the car park and walk down towards Wilmington village passing the ruinous remains of an old monastic priory. In a few minutes you will come to Wilmington church on your left. Should you, however, want a closer view of the chalky fellow first, the snaking path opposite the car park will take you to the foot of the Long Man though, in truth, he is best viewed from a distance.*

At Wilmington's Church of St Mary and St Peter you will encounter another giant – a great yew tree that is at least 1,600 years old. Great rivers of dark wood flow up the two main trunks of this majestic tree, and tall beams support it to prevent it falling over with the weight of its age. The church beside it is at least 1,000 years old, which means that when it was built this great yew was already mature. Wilmington's church is famous for its butterfly window, though look carefully and you'll see there are two featuring butterflies. The first you'll encounter entering the church on your right and contains a lone butterfly, a radiant sun, plants, a body of water and the words: 'Lift the stone and you shall find me, cleave the wood and you will see me.' While taken from one of the Gnostic Gospels of St Thomas, these words could easily be given a pagan interpretation too.

The more famous butterfly window is found round the corner in the north transept and features many butterflies, a bee and a fiery phoenix surrounding St Peter. (The first in your party to correctly identify all the insects in the glass deserves to be treated when you stop at the Long Man Inn!) Those taking this walk as a pilgrimage might want to make use of the church's pilgrim pot, 'for those walking the Cuckmere Pilgrim Path to share a written thought, reflections, poem or observation of their journey'.

❷ *Exiting the church look for the Cuckmere Pilgrim Path sign in the graveyard to both Alfriston via Milton Street and Alfriston via the Long Man. We are going to take the left-hand path via Milton Street and leave by the small iron gate.*

The Cuckmere Pilgrim Path was established in 2018 to connect seven churches in the area; its yellow and green signs use the traditional pilgrimage symbol of the scallop shell. The entire trail can be downloaded at cuckmerepilgrimpath.org.uk and covers about 12 miles (19 kilometres).

③ As you walk across the open field you will have fine views of the Long Man to your left and the 'Waste of Ondred' to your right – the great flat plain that lies between the South and North Downs. In spring the oilseed rape fields here dazzle with a vibrant yellow and are a delight to walk through (unless you are allergic to the pollen – in which case this would be hell). Where the path forks, continue on the pilgrim trail to the left. By the road look for a stile and telephone booth converted into a tiny library, they will lead you onwards.

Anyone familiar with Eric Ravilious's painting of the Long Man from 1939 will find little has changed in this landscape over 80 years, though it's hard not to read a wartime mood in the foregrounded barbed wire and greyness in Ravilious's portrayal of this part of Sussex.

④ Continue on the path until you see a large house on your right (Milton Court). Keep eyes peeled for a stile in the hedge; it is easy to miss when the greenery here is overgrown. Enter a tarmac road and pass the house and Milton Court Farm on your right. By now you should see the spire of Alfriston Church ahead of you. After 50 yards (45 metres) you will find the Pilgrim Path sign directing you to the footpath on your right. As you reach the outskirts of Alfriston you come to a road and bridge. Continue on the Pilgrim Path, keeping the river on your right, eventually crossing a lovely old white wooden bridge. At the bridge it's possible that the Devil will appear and, quite rationally, suggest beer, tea and large quantities of cakes from the various pubs and eateries in the village. Whether or not you resist him is your affair, though it's worth risking his ire to visit Alfriston Church, the next site on our pilgrim trail.

Often referred to as the Cathedral of the Downs, St Andrew's is a Grade I listed church built in the 1370s. The building is the shape of a Greek cross with a bell tower in the centre, evidenced by the ropes hanging in the middle of the building. The interior of this church has a calm simplicity to it and is a perfect place to gather your thoughts or conduct a simple ritual. Should you have had the foresight to pack a picnic for the walk, the many benches and greenery outside the church are a perfect spot to refresh – weather permitting.

⑤ Leaving the church, keep walking ahead to a cobbled twitten, passing the Congregational United Church and turning right onto the main road of the village. You may well want to spend some time here, not least because Alfriston has one of the best bookshops in England: Much Ado Books. Bags now laden with hardbacks, paperbacks and a plethora of cakes, fork left past the Smugglers Inn and keep going up the road. There is a distinct lack of a footpath for the next few hundred metres; thankfully this road has little traffic. Look for a wooden crucifix on the *wall halfway along this path and keep going until you reach Winton Street. Keep your eyes peeled here for a sign for Comp Barn and a chance to rejoin the Cuckmere Pilgrim Path down a gravel path to Berwick church, one of prettiest churches you will ever find.*

St Michael and All Angels Church was almost certainly built astride a barrow and close by a second one. Its interior is unique: in 1942 Duncan Grant, Vanessa Bell and Quentin Bell of the Bloomsbury Group began decorating the church and their paintings show Christ in the Downland landscape, echoing the words of William Blake when he asked: 'And did those feet in ancient time, walk upon England's mountains green? And did the Countenance Divine shine forth amongst those clouded hills?' Blake was referring to the legend that the young Jesus was brought to Britain by his uncle Joseph of Arimathea when he came here as a merchant, whereas Duncan Grant and the Bells have depicted Christ's birth by Mount Caburn beside Lewes. Here we see Christ as a baby with Mount Caburn in the background, shepherds bearing crooks unique to Sussex. Here too are pastoral scenes depicting the four seasons and the flowers and fruits of the earth.

In 2019 a major restoration project began, which means the old pews have been removed, the stonework has been cleaned, the floor has been re-tiled and the paintings have been restored. The result is a church filled with light and colour, helped by the clear windows that look out on to the old barrow beside the church. The original stained glass was blown out during the war and mercifully was not replaced. Most churches lock us away from the outside world – but here we can maintain our contact with the land. Sitting in here, two of the major sources of spiritual heritage that exist in these lands seem united as one – the early nature-based spirituality of pre-Christian times, together with the last few thousand years of Christian inheritance. Outside we can walk up on to the old barrow and look around at the graveyard and church, and feel that here, at least, we are not witnesses to the result of a foreign religion that has usurped a power spot of our native tradition. Here the transition from barrow-site to church and graveyard feels organic and natural.

When home, you can show others, and remind yourself of the beauty of this place by looking at the virtual tour offered at berwickchurch.org.uk

❻ *It took about an hour to walk to the church. Now you have about 50 minutes' walk back to the giant. Leave the church through the graveyard, keeping the Downs on the right, and go through a kissing gate into a field with a flint wall on your left. Head down into the right-hand corner of* the field and cross a stile. You should now be walking towards the Downs and will eventually reach Drusilla's Zoo. Watch out for any escaped meerkats running up your trouser leg. On the road beside the zoo turn left, walk up to the roundabout and take the recently created foot and cycle path that runs alongside the A27 Lewes Road towards Wilmington. Constant traffic and noise make this the least pleasant part of this walk but as the path continues it is separated a bit more from the road by hedges and trees. In about 15 minutes look for two footpath signs to your right. The first invites you to Milton Street. Ignore that and take the second. Follow the path that hugs the edge of the field, cross a road and rejoin the Pilgrim Path that wends its way towards Wilmington village. Our old friend the Long Man should have come into view by now too. You can either cut through to the main street to get directly to the Long Man Inn, or carry on up the path to the iron gate that leads you back into Wilmington churchyard.

Whether you find yourself walking past the yew having come up the village street, or whether you come to it through the churchyard, this ancient veteran tree will be patiently waiting for you, telling you that all is well and that all manner of things will be well. From here it a short walk to the car park or you can turn left and walk down into the village to reach the Long Man Inn which offers excellent food, accommodation and ale. More information about the mysterious Long Man can be found elsewhere in this book's Gazetteer (pages 14–18).

WALK 7

SACRED WATERS OF HASTINGS

ALEXANDRA PARK
TO ST HELEN'S WOODS

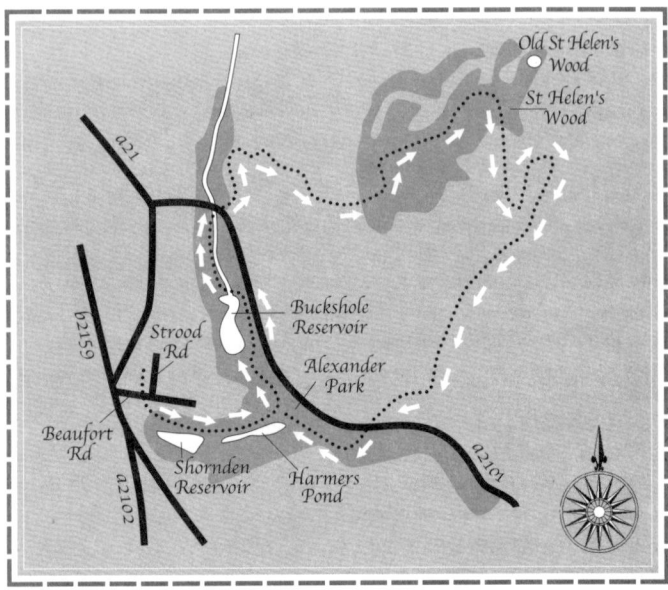

Summary
- **Start point:** North-west edge of Alexandra Park at Strood Road, south of Beaufort Road, parking spots are available on Strood Road, TN37 6PN
- **Distance:** Circular 7 miles (11 km)
- **Duration:** 3 hours
- **Description:** Woodland, waterways, small waterfalls, fairly flat, parts can be very muddy after rainfall
- **Refreshments:** None
- **Transport:** Car or train to St Leonard's with 20 minutes to start of the walk

A woodland trail through the outskirts of Hastings that takes in sacred springs, wells, mini waterfalls, the remains of an ancient church, a French mystic and a modern-day tale of the miraculous.

❶ *Walk south-east down Strood Road and at the bottom cross Beaufort Road to descend into the park down a tarmac lane. Within 110 yards (100 metres) or so we reach our first body of water – the*

Shornden Reservoir. With a keen eye for sunbathing terrapins and cormorants, continue along the left-hand edge of the reservoir. The path starts to descend beyond the reservoir. After a few hundred metres, and passing another two water bodies (the second being Harmers Pond), reach a green fingerpost and descend the stairs. At the bottom of the steps take a left, keeping the Pump House on your right and taking the lower descending path. Once past the miniature Park Woodland Railway keep left to continue on the path until you come to Dr McCabe's Well and Chalybeate Spring on your left.

Incorporated into Alexandra Park in 1878 the Chalybeate – meaning 'iron rich' – is accompanied by an old sign which suggests the waters have alleged health-giving properties but are 'foul-tasting'. Despite a faint eggy aftertaste these waters are, in fact, refreshing and with a metal tang, similar to the waters in Tunbridge Wells. The spring was named after the man who converted it into a well for public use and described it as having 'the advantage of not causing constipation'.

❷ *Continue on, curving to the right. Cross a short bridge over an ugly concrete water channel. Halfway up the path to the main road keep your eyes peeled for another unmarked well/spring on your right, with a more gentle sound. Reaching the steps to the main road veer left instead, to ascend to Buckshole Reservoir. Walk anti-clockwise around this body of water. About halfway round take the first right, and after a few yards take the left fork to reach the sign for Old Roar Gill and Coronation Wood.*

Swing a left after the sign and pass a wooden fence on your left and ascend to a bridge. As you continue keep as close to the ravine as you can. 'Access Closed' signs have been here for many years so you'll most likely have to take the stream's elevated path which will meet the lower path soon. There were a good deal of fallen trees on this path at time of publication so take care, especially if the ground is muddy.

Old Roar Gill is a 20-acre (8-hectare) deep narrow valley and woodland which probably formed around the same time as the North and South Downs. Old Roar is the name of the stream that runs through. It begins in North Hastings, runs all the way through the park to the sea and takes its name from the noise made by the larger of two waterfalls that lies further north. Dense with lush dark vegetation, tree roots, overhanging ferns and collapsed timber this whole area has a decidedly Jurassic Park feel. Don't be surprised to find Jeff Goldblum crashing through the ferns here mumbling, 'Life, uh, finds a way.'

❸ *Continue on the path with the gill stream on your right passing under the graffitied archway of a bridge. Soon you'll reach the first of our modest waterfalls then, after 20 feet (6 metres) or so, a second.*

Two circular pools sit at the base of the second waterfall. The vegetation here is rich with liverwort, lichen, red campions, primroses, violets and watercress. It also has a 'protective' oak, precariously lurching overhead amongst the sandstone and mudstone. In Russian mythology water witches were said to listen to the sound of running water as a form of divination, hearing words emanating out of the white noise. You might like to practise this by simply closing your eyes, clearing your mind and thinking about who might win the next Grand National.

❹ *Pass through the old Victorian gateposts and continue on to a wooden bridge, crossing the gill stream and up some stairs to reach our third waterfall, which despite being the biggest so far is named Little Roar.*

Don't be intimidated by the viewing platform here. Get up close to Little Roar and enjoy the natural amplification of the sound of the cascading water. You might even like to cool your head under the waterfall. Fans of mudlarking may also like to scrutinise the stream bed too; occasional Victorian curios have been known to be found here, brought from higher up the valley.

❺ *Retrace your movements back to the ascending steps which take us out of this verdant paradise into suburbia. When you meet the tarmac road, take a left up Ghyllside Avenue then right along Hickman Way. At the end, swing left up Grange Avenue, right along Ghyllside Way, left uphill on Parkstone Road then take the second right into Sheerwater Crescent. Follow the road as it curves to the left, pass two right turnings, then turn right onto a brown concrete road that brings you out at Willowbed Walk. Turn immediately right towards the footpath into St Helen's Woods, preparing not to enter the woods but to veer left into the field.*

Stop here to enjoy the fine views of distant Hastings seafront and the sea beyond before you. If you've brought a flask of coffee or tea with you, now's the time for a hearty swig; this next part is where you could get lost, so you need to stay focused.

❻ *Go left through a kissing gate into a field. Bear left to descend to the left-hand corner of the field, into the woods and down some steps which lead to a wooden chicane gate. Going through this, you will emerge into a meadowland of yarrow, fleabane and buttercups. Turn left on the path running horizontally towards the top left-hand corner of the field to a metal kissing gate. To the right of the kissing gate a couple of houses can be seen. Through the kissing gate follow the path to the top of the stairs to reach St Helen's Wood Road. Follow St Helen's Wood Road to the right with house sign numbers 47–57. Once you have passed all the houses and have fields on each side, pass the duck pond with a duck kennel in its centre on your left. Then swing left over a stile into a field which makes for a perfect spot for a picnic on a warm, dry day. Halfway up ascend right to a bench at the top right-hand edge of the field. To the right of the bench pass through a kissing gate into the woodland again, bearing slightly left to reach a gap in a metal fence. Go through, turn left, then immediately right onto a path by a wooden overlapping fence to your right. After 11 yards (10 metres) look for a small plank on the left over a small gully. Walk the plank and ascend through the woods, passing under one fallen beech tree. Keep going until you see a body of water on your right. Follow the path clockwise around the water keeping it on your right. Soon you will arrive at the lost spring of St Helen's Woods.*

This sacred spring was unearthed by local artist Mark Golding in the noughties after his son Gus was diagnosed with a rare and potentially deadly lung disease. In a 'herbal-induced' heightened state of consciousness Mark communicated his anxieties to the spirits of St Helen's Woods and came to understand that the area contained a blocked spring. 'Unblock the spring and you'll unblock your son's diseased lungs', was how he came to interpret the messages he was receiving. Working for weeks on end Mark completely unearthed what you see before you, and took the waters to his hospitalised son for a year. He survived. (Though, for Gus at least, the doctors and their medicine played their part too!)

Take your time to explore this area. Drink the waters from the spring. The circular pool below the spring is large enough for bathing, baptism and complete immersion. Look for the spring's mighty guardian oak and a beech tree to the right, into which is carved the word 'alchemy'. Since its unearthing this area has been regularly used for rites and rituals, evidenced by a 'pow-wow' circle of logs; young yew trees in pots, ritual offerings, candle stubs and ribbons.

An old tradition of sleeping by wells or springs for divination from dreams has been practised by some here, too.

Fans of the dark arts might be interested to know that a couple of hundred metres from here the 'Great Beast' and occultist Aleister Crowley lived out his autumn years in a boarding house, Netherwood. Apparently, he passed his time sitting quietly doing Baphomet-themed jigsaws and listening to *I'm Sorry I Haven't a Cult* on the wireless.

❼ *Retrace your steps under the fallen beech tree, re-cross the plank and turn left continuing on the main path, eyes peeled for an old Victorian drinking fountain half buried amongst the foliage. Continue to Dunclutha Road and go down it. Turn left into Friar's Way, and then left again to* climb Elphistone Road. Finally turn left at De Chardin Drive into Centurion Rise and then right into Ore Place to our last sacred location: the remnants of Old St Helen's Church.

Little remains of the seminary and abbey that once stood here, though local road names clearly allude to this once being a great place of pilgrimages. The lost spring of St Helen's Woods was once part of the abbey grounds too.

St Helen's Church still retains its impressive bell tower. Look for the writing in the ceiling on what look like strips of polished slate. While not easily legible, the word 'sacred' can be seen amongst the text.

In 1908 the Seminary welcomed a young man who would become its star pupil — 24-year-old Pierre Teilhard de Chardin, a French Christian mystic and philosopher who remained here for four years working on ideas that merged scientific, philosophical and theological knowledge. De Chardin is best known for developing the concept of the noosphere. Along with the atmosphere and biosphere the planet, he argued, has evolved a noosphere – an immaterial realm of ideas and creativity, the highest known stage of a planet's evolution.

❽ *Retrace your steps to Elphistone Road. Continue down it for about ½ mile (0.8 kilometres) passing Hastings United Football Club on your left. Soon after, veer right onto Down's Road for a mile as the road becomes St Helen's Park Road. At a crossroads with a church on the corner, turn right onto St Helen's Crescent. Take the second on the right into a dead-end cul-de-sac. Keep on the left pavement to find a brick walled pathway to the left of some black-and-white timbered flats. This emerges onto St Helen's Road at a pedestrian crossing. Cross the road, turn right and immediately left to head down Dortrecht Way. At the end of this road, take a path to the right to re-enter Alexandra Park. Continue keeping to the left-hand paths, you will see Hastings Peace Garden, to your right on the other side of a small stream – a less than holy holey stone and a giant feather on a park bench.*

❾ *Soon you'll head up an ascending left-hand path. Reach a wide stone track – sometimes used as a car park – turn right here and when you see the body of water (Harmers Pond), ignore the first left and take the second, keeping the water on your left-hand side. This is where you rejoin the first stages of the walk so you will be retracing your steps from here. Keeping to the right-hand side of Shornden Reservoir, bear right near the top of the reservoir and then left to ascend onto the path that will take you back to Strood Road.*

WALK 8

THE OCCULT MYSTERIES OF SUSSEX

STEYNING & CHANCTONBURY RING

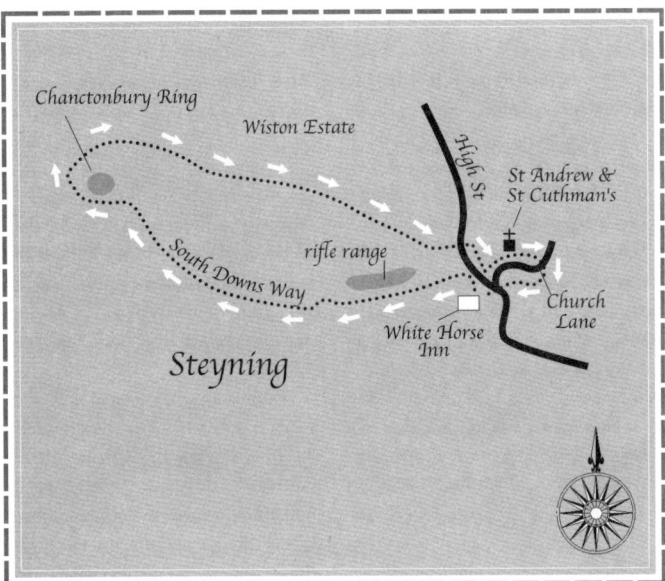

Summary
- **Start point:** The White Horse inn, Steyning BN44 3YE
- **Distance:** Circular 6 miles (10 km)
- **Duration:** 3–4 hrs
- **Description:** An invigorating walk that takes in not only open Downland, sweeping vistas and dappled paths, but introduces you to a fascinating town with many magical associations
- **Refreshments:** The White Horse or eateries and inns in Steyning
- **Transport:** Car or bus to Steyning

A satisfying 3–4 hour walk that begins and ends in the picturesque town of Steyning which, unbelievably now, was once a thriving sea port. Equally unlikely – for such a pretty, tranquil place – are Steyning's occult connections. On his *Chanctonbury Rings* album (2019) author Justin Hopper describes Steyning as, 'That strange town so full of spirits one could hardly move.' Exactly who and what they are will be revealed as this walk progresses. You can visit Steyning's special sites that we recommend either at the start of the walk or as we present it here – after refreshment at one of Steyning's inns.

❶ *Starting from The White Horse inn, where two ancient holy wells are somewhat hidden beneath vegetation-rich glass covers outside the building, walk away from the High Street up Sheep Pen Lane, take the first right at Whitehorse Square leading to Charlton Street, then left just before the police station. Go through the car park of the cricket club and cross the playing field diagonally until you reach a kissing gate at the far corner of the field. Here you join a stone track that leads uphill, past allotments on your left. Keep going up this main path for another 20 minutes or so passing the rifle range on your right and journeying through Steyning Combe as you ascend.*

❷ *The path continues uphill, until you reach the edge of woodland. At the Steyning Downland Scheme marker post take a right onto the South Downs Way link route. Follow the path upwards. At the top of the hill bear right along the stone path with a fenced field to your left. Keep going with the fence running to your left. After ½ mile (0.8 kilometres) or so it snakes round southwards towards the sea. Continue on it to join the South Downs Way heading west. After 1 mile (1.6 kilometres) you reach Chanctonbury Ring. Head into the Ring and enjoy its atmosphere.*

Although like Hollingbury and Cissbury, Chanctonbury was once a hillfort, there is a markedly different atmosphere here. This may be simply due to the presence of so many beech trees, planted in 1760 by landowner Charles Goring, making it less windswept and fostering more flora and fauna than on the other more exposed Sussex hillforts. After the hurricane of 1987, however, many were lost in the storm – now seemingly replaced by ash and sycamore – but this did give archaeologists the chance to do more excavations of two temples on the site, built here during the Roman period, between about 50 and 400 CE.

Religious and magical activities carried out here over the centuries have also helped Chanctonbury cultivate an altogether more numinous feeling. It's certainly a place for meditation and magical rites. Just don't run seven times backwards around the Ring or you might meet the Devil, according to folklore. Or he might simply offer you a bowl of soup in exchange for your soul – a perfectly reasonable proposition if you happen to be hungry.

Prominent author and specialist on the Grail mysteries and Celtic spirituality, John Matthews, has spoken of his initiation into a magical group he stumbled upon one night in the Ring when he was a teenager, who dated their origin to the Middle

Ages; others have recorded evidence of magical rituals being performed here in modern times. UFO sitings and paranormal phenomena, such as the appearance of ghosts known as the Midnight Druid and the White-Bearded Saxon, all contribute to its reputation as a place of power.

And what other Sussex hilltop could boast being the subject of an entire psychogeographically themed album of hauntings? In their 2019 record *Chanctonbury Rings*, author Justin Hopper and musician Sharron Kraus create a heady blend of folktronica and spoken word with Hopper describing the location as 'the thin place on my map. It is there that dead friends visit and dead voices gather'.

It's also worth remembering that not everything that goes bump in the night is a ghost. In his book *The Old Ways* (2012), nature writer Robert Macfarlane describes a terrifying encounter he once had here sleeping alone amongst the trees and claimed to have been awakened by the unidentifiable unearthly screeching of something circling above him. Don't tell him we said so but that does sound suspiciously like a barn owl.

❸ *When you're ready to leave, go to the western side of the Ring and facing west and looking down the hillside you'll see a fence running along with a gate that leads towards a path that slopes down the hill. It's a fairly steep descent here and when wet can be treacherously slippery. Continue until you meet the path that runs along the foot of the hill. Turn right on to this lower path and follow for a couple of miles.*

This lower pathway – that hugs the side of the Downs and passes the mysterious Wilton Park at Wiston House used by government think-tanks – is lovely to walk along in spring and summer when dappled sunlight lights the path and myriad butterflies and moths flit along it. After heavy rain however it can be a squelchy endurance test.

❹ *On reaching Mouse Lane turn right for 10 minutes then left onto the public footpath that passes St Columba Community Farm and eventually takes you all the way back to Steyning High Street.*

Along the High Street, look out for the Chequer Inn, mentioned in Hilaire's Belloc's *The Four Men* (1911), an account of his pilgrimage across Sussex, and take some time to browse in the wonderful Steyning Bookshop.

❺ *When you get to The White Horse inn, take a left down Church Street and when you get to the church, follow the street round to the left of the church and look out for the elegant 18th-century Chantry House at number 34.*

The poet and member of the magical Order of the Golden Dawn W.B. Yeats (1865–1939) lived here briefly at the end of his life and wrote some of his most important late poetry there; the painter Gluck (1895–1978) lived there later, painting most of her best-known work in the studio.

❻ *Walk back to St Andrew and St Cuthman's Church.*

This Norman church stands on foundations of a church that was probably here as early as the 8th century. It was the centre of the cult of St Cuthman who famously wheeled his disabled mother in a sort of wheelbarrow from somewhere in the west. When the barrow broke down he decided to found a church where this happened. Alfred the Great's father was originally buried here, and as soon as you enter the church, you'll notice a gravestone leaning upright. It is so ancient it might be pre-Christian. The dowser Hamish Miller describes in *The Book of English Magic* (2009) how every time he touched this stone he felt 'a jolt of energy and meaning'. Eventually he hugged the stone and felt himself flying with no limit to time and space. He believes the stone is carved with runes symbolising Mystery, Forgiveness and Harmony. The interior of the church is no less intriguing. The nave is high – with upper windows forming a clerestory, bringing in light from above. This in itself is an unusual feature in a 12th-century parish church, but add in the decorated nave arcades and the effect is one of tremendous solemnity and grandeur. Now, as in most churches, the stonework is bare, and we have to imagine what it was like when it was first built. All these arches, each carved with different shapes and decorated with human or animal heads, were originally painted in bright colours. With sunshine pouring through the stained-glass windows and with the entire nave ablaze with colour, congregations were lifted into a celestial world in preparation for receiving the eucharist. As the printed guide to the church suggests, the master mason here must have had in mind the Book of the Apocalypse which describes the Heavenly Jerusalem as having walls of jasper, garnished with precious stones: sapphires, chalcedony, emeralds.

❼ *On leaving the church, retrace your steps up Church Street heading towards the High Street but keep your eyes open for Vine Cottage on your right, between Saxon Cottage and the Model Bakery.*

One of the great occult practitioners of early 20th-century England, the poet Victor Neuburg (1883–1940) once lived and worked here, publishing books of poems and non-fiction, all printed on a hand-cranked press, and issued under the imprint of the Vine Press.

In the early years of the 20th century Neuburg became the friend and lover of the magician Aleister

Crowley (1875–1947), and together – in the Algerian desert – they performed the very first of Crowley's rites of sex magic, which later brought him such notoriety. Neuburg later broke with Crowley and moved to Steyning where he continued to write poetry. Here in this tranquil setting he set up the Vine Press, married, and raised a son.

A very short walk will take you back to the starting point of your trek. Should you want one final adventure in this area, visiting another shrine to a very different early 20th-century visionary, see details for Vera Pragnell's Sanctuary on pages 46–47.

WALK 9

A PLEIADES PILGRIMAGE

UP ON THE LEWES DOWNS

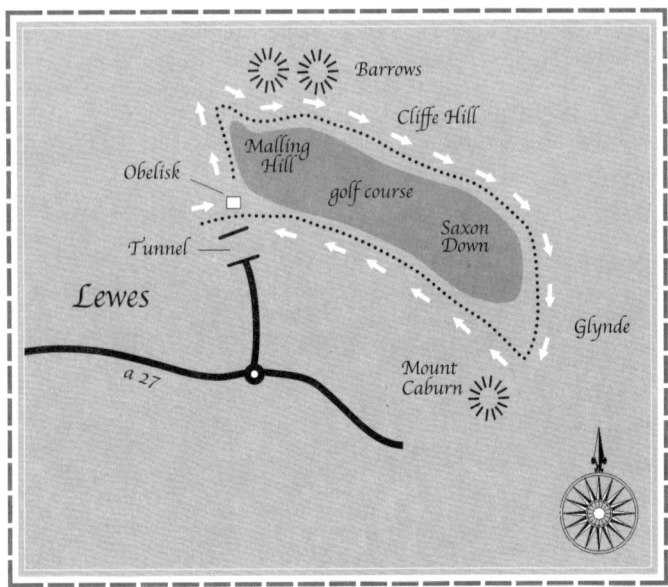

Summary

- **Start point:** The start of Chapel Hill, at its junction with South Street, Lewes, BN7 2BT
- **Distance:** Circular 5 miles (8 km)
- **Duration:** 3 hours
- **Description:** An invigorating walk that is fairly challenging, with an elevation gain of 1,266 feet (386 metres), visiting tumuli and a hillfort, with panoramas of open Downland and the sea beyond
- **Refreshments:** The Café du Jardin is a few paces away from the start and end point, behind Pastorale Antiques in Malling Street. The Snowdrop Inn is 5 minutes' walk in the other direction, along South Street
- **Transport:** Lewes Station is 15 minutes' walk from the start point

A 3-hour walk that involves trekking up steps and paths that climb and then descend almost 1,312 feet (400 metres), so not for those with dodgy knees or who get out of breath easily. You will be amply rewarded for your efforts, though, by visiting five of what may have been a complex of seven sacred summits that uncannily mirror the pattern of the Seven Sisters of the Pleiades star cluster in the constellation of Taurus. (Read more about this on pages 10–11.)

❶ Starting from outside one of the best children's bookshops in the country, Bags of Books, walk up Chapel Hill, until the houses finish on your left side. Leave the road here, turning to your left and then rather than taking the footpath that leads up to the Cuilfail Estate, take the right fork up through the wood and walk up the steps that lead up the hill. When you get to the golf course, walk along the left-hand edge, passing the Obelisk, a memorial to the 17 Protestant martyrs who were burnt to death during the Catholic reign of Queen Mary I, 1553–1558.

❷ The path continues until you reach the boundary of the golf course. Go through the gate in the corner of the fences, which takes you into the Malling Down Nature Reserve. Follow the path to your right which tracks along the side of the Coombe, and leads towards Malling Hill. At the bottom of the Coombe you can see a strip of allotments. Soon you are walking around the fecund stomach of the 'Fat-bellied Woman', as this hillside was called by some of the old folk in Lewes. Up where her breasts would be are two round barrows on the horizon known locally as the 'Camel's Humps'. Keep on the path and you will get to the first summit: Malling Hill. Just a few metres west from the top, you will find the traces of a barrow. And a little way to the east you will find a dew pond.

In accordance with the suggestion that these Lewes hills may have been sensed in Neolithic times as in a mysterious sympathy with the stars of the Pleiades, it is here that you might be able to magically tune into one of them: Atlas.

Standing here, look beyond the town of Lewes which lies below you to the north-west. On the ridge above the town you will see the distinctive scar of the Offham chalk-pit. Above here was a Neolithic causewayed enclosure – a great tribal meeting place. And it is along this ridge that the sun, at the summer solstice, appears to 'bounce down' the horizon (see page 36).

❸ Walking east, you come to a dew pond – head for the next summit, Cliffe Hill. Following the track for about 55 yards (0.5. kilometres), you will then need to deviate a few metres from the path to stand on the next – our second summit, tuning in perhaps to the inspiration of Alcyone.

❹ Back on the path, head south-east towards the third summit, about ⅔ mile (1 kilometre) on, of Saxon Down. Here the vista changes as you look down, not on Lewes but towards the east, with the Glyndebourne wind turbine clearly visible, powering one of the finest opera houses in the world. Here it is the star Maia who might perhaps whisper to you. Then press onward, towards the most spectacular part of this walk.

❺ After about a ⅔ mile (1 kilometre) you come to another slight summit, the land rising a little to face woodland below known as Glynde Holt. Lacking an official name, let's call this Glynde Hill — as suggests Andy Stirling, Professor of Science and Technology Policy at Sussex University, who has proposed the idea that the ancients may have built their many barrows in this region because of its uncanny resonance with the Pleiades cluster. The star Taygeta is located exactly at this point — our fourth summit — if we follow the Stirling scheme.

6 *Continuing on, you follow the path due south for ⅔ mile (1 kilometre) or so, passing two perfectly-formed round barrows to your left.* Here you are on top of the world. The hillside sweeps down to your left with broad vistas of fields and woods laid out below. To your right are the folds of hills and coombes that eventually lead back to Lewes. But ahead of you is a splendid sight: the ancient hillfort of Mount Caburn, approached seemingly from the rear, with the domain it surveys spread out beyond and below it: drained flatland with two conspicuous rises which in ancient times would have been islands amongst the marshes. And all across this panorama lies the sinuous path of the Ouse as it runs from the sea on the horizon before it reluctantly flows into the strait-jacket it was given in the early 19th century when it was artificially channelled into a straight line as it nears Lewes.

Climb up through the entrance-way carved out of the bank to gain access to this magnificent hillfort, our fifth summit. To your left you'll see a pit that is said to mark where a roundhouse once stood. Atop the hill you understand why the Belgae tribe chose this spot. Why waste time eating waffles in Brussels or Bruges when you can nip across the Channel and get a view like this?

The curious and rebellious trekker might choose to take a risk now to trespass across private land to reach the sixth and seventh summits of this sacred landscape. Climbing a gate, they would reach first Ranscombe Hill that Stirling links to the star Electra. Then, with a clear view of the artificial embankment possibly built in a hurry as the Romans invaded and never finished, they would walk down the slope to climb a barbed-wire fence to reach the Round-the-Down hillside that Stirling links to the star Merope. Here, at Machine Bottom just above the Light Bros scrap metal dealers yard in Southerham, lie the remains of an unusually large round barrow excavated in the 1970s.

Since we cannot recommend such a risky adventure, our walk continues along publicly accessible land:

7 *From Mount Caburn, retrace your steps for 437 yards (400 metres) or so until you reach the footpath that leads west, back towards the golf course. This takes you down about ⅔ mile (1 kilometre) to Oxteddle Bottom. You then take a right by the dew pond to Bible Bottom, so named because of a square earthwork that could be confused — from a distance and with the* *aid of several pints of the local Harvey's ale — for a giant open bible. Keep going — it's pretty steep here, then at the T-junction of paths take a left and enter the smooth grassland of the golf course.*

As you walk west on the home stretch now, ducking the occasional golf ball, you might notice after about 500 yards (457 metres), a cluster of fine birch trees, in the area of the 14th hole. Peculiarly, and rather magically, it is only from this spot that you can see all seven summits of the Pleiades hills. (See page 89).

❽ *Follow the path as it turns right now to take you home. You can either walk down the tarmacked road here which feeds into Chapel Hill, or take the more attractive path across the grass that takes you back to the often-muddy rough stairway that takes you back down into Chapel Hill.*

TIPS FOR SAFE WALKING

*'I took a walk in the woods
and came out taller than the trees.'*

HENRY DAVID THOREAU

Preparations

Seasonally appropriate clothing really enhances the enjoyment of walking – boots and water- and wind-proof coats in winter, walking sandals and a hat for shade from bright sunlight in summer (and winter when the low winter sun can be very bright). High-factor suncream and first aid – plasters at the very least – are also recommended.

Provisions

Take a flask of hot drink, a bottle of water and a nourishing snack. Even if there is a refreshment possibility on the route, pubs can close... Having some food and drink with you can also reduce anxiety if you get lost.

Rest

A piece of foam or bubble wrap weighs next to nothing and allows you to sit down even when the ground is wet.

Maps

We strongly recommend that you take a map. While heroic efforts have been made to make our maps and written directions accurate, things do change on the ground: footpath signs blow down (or are 'lost' by landowners); pubs are given new names; fences appear; trees and hedges are cut down; and bridges, even roads sometimes, close or move. However good our map may be, if by chance you come off the route, an OS map allows you to find your way back. It also means that you can tell someone exactly where you are in case of an emergency. We recommend the Explorer range which has a scale of 1 in 25,000 (2.5 inches to the mile or 1 cm to 0.25 km) – large enough to show field boundaries and footbridges.

High-tech

Mobile phones can be reassuring, but they can also be out of range. Global Positioning Systems (GPS) are quite reliable but do not always work in dense woodland.

Orientation

Take time to get properly oriented at the beginning – it is surprisingly easy to set off in the wrong direction – and reorient yourself at intervals when you reach unmistakable features. Turning the map to suit your sense of direction may be mocked but many people find it helps.

Keeping on track

Following footpaths shown on the map is not (normally) difficult. It helps if you check the direction a fingerpost is indicating as you climb each stile and look for signs of the path ahead – even a little-used grassy path is usually discernible. Remembering that footpaths have stiles and bridle paths have gates can help. It is worth noticing contour lines too, not just to see where the hills are going to be, but to check that you are where you think you are.

Intermediate tech

Hiking poles or a sturdy stick (or two) can help on hilly walks and slippery ground and will increase the distance you can walk comfortably.

Buses & trains

We have included linear walks because they increase the variety of terrain you can cover and offer the particular satisfaction of walking from one distinct place to another. We hope that you will explore public transport possibilities, thereby supporting local bus and train services. Check public transport information before setting off – if the bus or train service is infrequent it makes sense to finish a walk where there is a pub or a tea shop, and the linear routes take this into account.

Weather

It can be markedly colder on high ground, even on the relatively modest heights of the Sussex hills. There are also climatic differences on exposed coasts: Rye Bay is always considerably colder than other sections of the Sussex coast. BBC News 24 weather reports use rainfall radar and are usually accurate.

More weather

Choose your walk in relation to the weather: winds on top of the Downs can be ferocious and the rain can feel like needles. A linear walk with a good following wind might be fun. Mists can greatly reduce visibility (and temperature) on the coast when it is clear, warm and sunny up on the High Weald. If the hills have 'got their hats on' – i.e. the Downland tops such as Firle Beacon or Chanctonbury appear to be shrouded in cloud – it will be much wetter than you think when you get to the top and will probably rain soon at lower levels.

ACKNOWLEDGEMENTS & RESOURCES

SERENA MITCHELL for the excellent features on St Andrew's Church and St Lewinna.

SARAH JANES for mapping out the Sacred Waters of Hastings walk.

DAISY MACDONALD & NIGEL FARROW for trialling the walk in gruelling conditions.

ALEXANDRA LOSKE for providing us with insider knowledge on the Meeting House.

ANDY STIRLING for taking us on an adventure, and a trespass, to explore the seven summits above Lewes.

ANNE RUPERT for joining us on all the walks and sharing her wisdom.

Handy Apps

OS MAPS & ALLTRAILS will help you find your way and plan new adventures.

POCKET GUIDE MEGALITHS & MEGALITHIC EXPLORER give information on megalithic sites.

Walking with Others

THE BRITISH PILGRIMAGE TRUST
britishpilgrimage.org

THE GATEKEEPER TRUST
gatekeeper.org.uk arrange pilgrimages, walks and workshops to explore the sacred landscape of Britain.

Books

20 Sussex Churches, Simon Watney (Snake River Press, 2007)

Britain's Pilgrim Places, Nick Mayhew Smith & Guy Hayward (Lifestyle Press, 2021)

Curiosities of East Sussex, David Arscott (SB Publications, 1991)

Curiosities of West Sussex, David Arscott (SB Publications, 1993)

A Dictionary of Sussex Folk Medicine, Andrew Allen (Countryside Books, 1995)

The Druid Way: A Journey Through an Ancient Landscape, Philip Carr-Gomm (Oak Tree Press, 2024). Weaves history, folklore, Druidry, spirituality and psychology into the story of a walk from a sacred hill in Lewes, Sussex, to the giant chalk hill-figure of the Long Man of Wilmington.

Sussex Folk Tales for Children, Xanthe & Robin Knight (The History Press, 2018)

The Traditional Culture of Sussex: Both Sides of the Downs, Geoff Doel (Fonthill Media, 2020)

The Wilmington Giant, Rodney Castleden (Turnstone Press, 1983)

INDEX

Adsdean Down Tumuli,
  Kingley Vale   37–38
Alexandra Park, Hastings   78–79, 82
Alfriston   73–75

Barrows   34–38, 57, 60, 76, 90
Belloc, Hillaire   11, 28, 51, 85
Beltane   15
Berwick Church *see* St Michael and
  All Angels Church, Berwick
Blake, William   48–49, 51, 76
Blake's Cottage, Felpham   48–49
Bloomsbury Set   73, 76

Carpenter, Edward   47
Castleden, Rodney   17, 35–36
Cerne Abbas Giant, Dorset
                                 15, 16, 17
Chalk figures   14–18
Chalybeate springs   22, 72, 79
Chanctonbury Ring   29, 32, 83–87
Chattri, the   63–64
Chidham Peninsula, Chichester   27
Chithurst Buddhist Monastery
                              39–40, 66–68
Christian Sussex   6–8, 43, 47
Cissbury Ring   9, 56–58
Cittaviveka *see* Chithurst Buddhist
  Monastery
Clayton Tunnel   65
Coombes Church, Lancing   42–43
Crowley, Aleister   47, 50–51, 81, 87
Cuckmere Pilgrim Path   29, 73–77

Devil's Dyke   6, 9, 19, 29
Devil's Humps, Kingley Vale
                                 38, 59–62

Devil's Jumps, Treyford   38
Ditchling   19, 32
Druidry   8, 14, 18, 20–21,
                      24–25, 26, 32, 36–37

Eastbourne   23, 29, 44
Elm trees   25–26
  The Gilded Elm   26
English Martyr's Church,
  Goring-by-Sea   41

Field Museum, Kingley Vale   60
Fulking Spring   23

Goldstone, Hove   19–20
Gurdy Stone, Kingston   21

Hamblin, Henry Thomas
  ('Saint of Sussex')   51–52
Hammer Wood, Chithurst   39, 67–68
Harmers Pond, nr Hastings   78–79
High Rocks, nr Tunbridge
  Wells   69–72
Highdown Gardens, Worthing   56–58
Hillforts   31–32, 34, 56–58, 67, 90
  Chanctonbury Ring Hillfort   83
  Cissbury Ring Hillfort   56
  Hollingbury Camp   32
  Mount Caburn Hillfort   88
Hollingbury Camp   9, 32–33
Holywell Eastbourne   23
Hopper, Justin   11, 12, 83, 85

Italian Gardens, Eastbourne   23

Jefferies, Richard   51, 64

[95]

THE LONG MAN & FRIENDS

Kingley Vale   37–38, 59–62
Kingston   19, 21

Lammas (Lughnasadh)   35
Lewes   6, 10–11, 12, 34
  Lewes Downs (walk)   88–91
  Lewes Priory   35, 37
  Lewes Tump   35–37
  Mount Caburn, Lewes
        11, 24, 37, 76, 90
Lewinna, St   43–45
Ley lines   11–12, 16
Litlington White Horse   18
Long Man Inn   8, 18, 25, 73, 74, 77
Long Man of Wilmington
        8, 10, 11, 14–18, 73–77
Lullington   7

Meeting House, Sussex University
  Campus   46
Mount Caburn, Lewes
        11, 24, 37, 76, 90

Neolithic
        10, 28, 29, 34, 37, 57, 60, 89
Neuburg, Victor   47, 86–87

Oak trees   26–27
  The Queen Elizabeth Oak   26–27
  Norman Oak, Petworth Park   27
Old Steine (Victoria) Fountain,
  Brighton   20–21

Pleiades   10–11, 88–91
Pragnell, Vera   46–47, 51
Pyecombe   63–65

Ravilious, Eric   75

St Andrew and St Cuthman's
  Church, Steyning   86–87
St Andrew's Church, Alfriston   75
St Andrew's Church, Bishopstone
        43–45

St Botolph's Church, Hardham   42
St Helen's Woods   78–82
St Mary and St Peter's Church,
  Wilmington   73, 74
St Michael and All Angels Church,
  Berwick   7, 76
St Richard's Church, Burton Park   45
Samhain   15, 25

Sanctuary, Washington   46–47
Silbury Hill, Avebury   10, 28, 35–37
Solstices   8–9, 11, 18, 54
South Downs Way
        15, 28, 29, 38, 64, 84
Steyning   83–87
Steyning Stone   86
Stirling, Andy   10, 90
Sussex Ouse Valley Way   30

Tumps/tumuli   34–38

Uncumber, St   45

Valiente, Doreen   52–53

Walking tips   92–93
Waste of Ondred   6, 54, 57, 75
Watkins, Alfred   11, 16
White Horse Inn, Steyning   83–85
Wicca   52–53
  Eightfold Wheel of the Year   18, 53
Wilfrid, St   6, 43
Wilgefortis, St   45
Wilmington   73–77
  Long Man Inn   8, 18, 25, 73, 74, 77
  Long Man of Wilmington
        8, 10, 11, 14–18, 73–77
Windover Hill   15

Yew trees   24–25, 61, 62, 74
  Coldwaltham Yew   25
  Crowhurst Yew   25
  Kingley Vale Yew Forest   59–62
  Wilmington Yew   25, 74